STATUTORY RULES OF NORTHERN IRELAND

1994 No. 243

BUILDING REGULATIONS

Building Regulations (Northern Ireland) 1994

Made . . . . 28th June 1994

Coming into operation . . . . . . 28 November 1994

ARRANGEMENT OF REGULATIONS

Part A: Interpretation and general

Part B: Materials and workmanship

GU00566474

1

SCHEDULES

The Department of the Environment, in exercise of the powers conferred by Articles 3, 5(1), (2) and (3), 15(2) and (7), 16(1) and (2) and 17(1) and (2) of, and paragraphs 1 to 7, 9 to 13 and 17 to 22 of Schedule 1 to, the Building Regulations (Northern Ireland) Order 1979**(a)** and now vested in it**(b)** and of every other power enabling it in that behalf, hereby makes the following regulations:–

(a) S.I. 1979/1709 (N.I. 16)
(b) S.I. 1982/338 (N.I. 6) Art. 5 and Sch 1 Part 11

PART A

Interpretation and general

A1   Citation and commencement

These regulations may be cited as the Building Regulations (Northern Ireland) 1994 and shall come into operation on 28 November 1994.

A2   Interpretation

(1)   In these regulations—

AGRICULTURE includes horticulture, fruit growing, seed growing, dairy farming, breeding and keeping of livestock, fish farming, the use of land as grazing land, meadow land, market gardens and nursery grounds, and the use of land for woodlands where that use is ancillary to the farming of land for other agricultural purposes;

BOUNDARY means, in relation to a building, the boundary of the land belonging to the building and, except for the purposes of Part R, such land shall be deemed to include any abutting part of any street, canal or river but only up to the centre line thereof; and BOUNDARY OF THE PREMISES shall be construed so as to include any such part to the same extent;

BUILDING WORK means the erection of a building, the structural alteration or extension of a building (including work in connection with the making of a material change of use) or the provision of a service or fitting;

CONSERVATORY means a part or extension of a building attached to and having a door giving access from the attached building and having not less than three- quarters of the area of its roof and not less than one-half of the area of its external walls made of translucent material;

CONSTRUCTION PRODUCTS DIRECTIVE means European Council Directive 89/106/EEC on the approximation of laws, regulations and administrative provisions of the Member States relating to construction products(a);

(a)   OJ No L40, 11.2.89, p 12

DEPARTMENT means the Department of the Environment;

DISTRICT COUNCIL means the district council having the function of enforcing these regulations;

DRAIN means any pipe or drain used solely for or in connection with the rain – water or foul water drainage of one building or of any buildings or yards appurtenant to buildings within the same curtilage;

DWELLING (except in Part E) means a house, flat or maisonette and includes any accommodation therein of not more than 50 m^2 in total floor area, forming part of the dwelling and used by a resident of the dwelling for the purposes of any business, profession or calling;

EDUCATIONAL BUILDING means —

(a) a university;
(b) a school or college of education within the meaning of the Education and Libraries (Northern Ireland) Order 1986**(a)**; or
(c) any other institution providing facilities for further education under Article 27 of that Order.

ENACTMENT includes any instrument made under any statute;

EEA STATE means a State which is a Contracting Party to the Agreement on the European Economic Area signed at Oporto on 2 May 1992 as adjusted by the Protocol signed at Brussels on 17 March 1993, but until that Agreement comes into force in relation to Liechtenstein does not include that State;

EUROPEAN TECHNICAL APPROVAL means a favourable technical assessment of the fitness for use of a construction product for an intended use, issued for the purposes of the Construction Products Directive by a body authorised by a Member State to issue European Technical Approvals for those purposes and notified by that Member State to the European Commission;

FLOOR AREA means, in relation to any building or part of a building, the aggregate area of every floor in that building or part, calculated by reference to the finished internal faces of the walls enclosing the building or extension, or if at any point there is no such wall, by reference to the outermost edge of the floor;

GARAGE includes a carport;

GREENHOUSE means a building, constructed substantially of translucent material, which is ancillary to a dwelling, used mainly for growing plants and, where it is attached to the dwelling, is not entered from it;

(a) SI 1986 No 594 (NI 3)

HABITABLE ROOM means a room in any building (whether or not that building is or contains a dwelling) used or intended to be used for dwelling purposes, including any bedroom, but not any room used only for kitchen purposes;

HARMONIZED STANDARD means a standard established, as mentioned in the Construction Products Directive, by the European Standards Organisation on the basis of a mandate given by the Commission of the European Economic Community and published by the Commission in the Official Journal of the European Communities;

INSTITUTION means —

(a) a hospital, nursing home, home for old people or for children, school, or other similar establishment used as living accommodation or for the treatment, care or maintenance of people suffering from illness or mental or physical disability or handicap; and

(b) a place of lawful detention,

where people sleep on the premises;

KITCHEN PURPOSES means the purposes of preparing, storing, treating, cooking or manufacturing food or drink intended for human consumption or the cleansing of utensils or appliances which come into contact with such food or drink;

MATERIAL CHANGE OF USE (except in regulation A4) has the meaning assigned to it by regulation A9(1);

PARTIALLY EXEMPTED BUILDING means any part of a building described in Part A of Schedule 1;

PORCH means a single-storey enclosure providing protection to an access door to a building and having an external door or an opening to the external air;

PRIVATE SEWER means any part of a sewer, not being a public sewer, which serves two or more properties;

PROVISION OF A SERVICE OR FITTING in relation to any building includes the installation of any service or fitting to which these regulations apply or the alteration or the extension of any such service or fitting;

PUBLIC BUILDING means a building consisting of or containing—

(a) a theatre, public library, hall or other place of public resort;

(b) an educational building; or

(c) a place of public worship,

but a building is not to be treated as a place of public resort because it is, or it contains a shop, storehouse or warehouse, or is a dwelling to which members of the public are occasionally admitted;

SEWER includes all sewers, pipes or drains, other than a drain as defined in this regulation, and includes any apparatus used in connection with a sewer;

SHOP means—

(a) premises used for the retail of goods or services and includes premises—

    (i) used for the sale to members of the public of food or drink for consumption on or off the premises;

    (ii) used for retail sales by auction to members of the public;

    (iii) used to provide hairdressing or similar personal services to members of the public;

    (iv) where members of the public may take goods for repair or other treatment; and

    (v) where members of the public may go to hire an item; and

(b) premises used for wholesale self-selection trading;

SINGLE STOREY BUILDING means a building consisting of one storey only the floor of which is at or about the level of the finished surface of the ground adjoining the building;

SITE , in relation to a building, means the area of ground covered or to be covered by the building, including its foundations;

STATUTORY UNDERTAKING means an undertaking authorised by any enactment being a railway, road transport, air transport, water transport, inland navigation, dock or harbour undertaking, the Post Office Corporation or any undertaking for the generation, transmission or supply of electricity or gas;

STRUCTURAL ALTERATION means the execution of any work (other than the erection of a building and the provision of a service or fitting) to which the requirements of these regulations would apply if the work were part of a building being newly erected and includes the replacement of windows (other than replacement by ones having essentially similar features) and the insertion of material into a cavity in a wall of an existing building for the purpose of insulation;

SUBSTANTIVE REQUIREMENTS means the requirements of these regulations with respect to the design and construction of buildings and the provision of a service or fitting, as distinct from procedural requirements;

UNDER FORMER CONTROL —

(a) used in relation to any building, refers to a building the erection of which was—

    (i) completed before 1 October 1973;

      (ii) completed on or after 1 October 1973 in accordance with plans deposited with the district council before that date with or without any departures or deviations from those plans; or

      (iii) begun before but completed on or after 1 October 1973 (being a building the erection of which was exempt from compliance with the provisions of all relevant bye-laws in force immediately before that date); and

  (*b*) used in relation to any alteration or extension of a building or the provision of any service or fitting, refers to any such alteration, extension or provision which was—

      (i) completed before 1 October 1973;

      (ii) completed on or after 1 October 1973 in accordance with plans deposited with the district council before that date, with or without any departures or deviations from those plans; or

      (iii) begun before but completed on or after 1 October 1973 (being an alteration or extension or provision of a service or fitting which was exempt from compliance with the provisions of all relevant bye-laws in force immediately before that date);

WHOLLY EXEMPTED BUILDING means any building falling within one of the classes described in Part B of Schedule 1;

WINDOW means any sash, casement or other framing and associated glazing set in an opening in a wall or roof of a building; and

WORK OF PUBLIC UTILITY means a pipeline, gas holder, gas main, electricity supply line and supports, water main, public sewer or telephone line and supports.

(2) For the purposes of these regulations any of the following operations shall be deemed to be the erection of a building—

  (a) the re-erection of any building or part of a building when an outer wall of that building or (as the case may be) that part of a building has been pulled down or burnt down to within 3 metres of the surface of the ground adjoining the lowest storey of the building or of that part of the building;

  (b) the re-erection of any frame building or part of a frame building when that building or part of a building has been so far pulled down or burnt down as to leave only the framework of the lowest storey of the building or of that part of the building; and

  (c) the roofing over of any open space between walls or buildings.

(3) For the purpose of these regulations, the installation of a cesspool, septic tank or similar structure shall be treated as the provision of a service and not as the erection of a building.

(4) In these regulations any reference to a building shall extend to and include any part of a building, and any reference to the purpose for which a building is used shall extend to, include or mean the purpose for which it is intended to be used.

(5) Where in relation to a specific purpose, a European Council Directive prescribes a requirement in relation to a particular characteristic of a material, component or other manufactured product, or part thereof, then where that characteristic complies with that requirement, it shall be deemed to satisfy any requirement of these regulations insofar as it relates to that purpose.

And, accordingly, for the removal of doubt, it is hereby declared that products designed and manufactured in accordance with the requirements of a European Council Directive relating to a specific purpose do not have to comply with any standard or code of practice (British, international or other) prescribed or otherwise referred to in these regulations relating to any purpose covered by that Directive.

(6) In these regulations any reference to a British Standard or British Standard Code of Practice shall be construed as a reference to an appropriate British Standard or British Standard Code of Practice issued by the British Standards Institution and also to—

(a) a relevant harmonized standard or a relevant standard or code of practice of a national standards body, or equivalent body, of any European Economic State;

(b) any relevant international standard recognised for use in any EEA State;

(c) any appropriate, traditional procedures of manufacture of an EEA State where these are the subject of a written technical description sufficiently detailed to permit assessment of the goods or materials for the use specified; or

(d) a European Technical Approval issued in accordance with the Construction Products Directive (or, until procedures are available for the issue of such approvals, a specification sufficiently detailed to permit assessment):

Provided that the proposed standard, code of practice, specification, technical description or European Technical Approval provides, in use, equivalent levels of safety, suitability and fitness for purpose as that provided by the British Standard or British Standard Code of Practice.

(7) For the purposes of these regulations, any construction product (within the meaning of the Construction Products Directive) which bears an EC marking shall be treated as if it satisfied the requirements of any appropriate British Board of Agrément Certificate, British Standard or British Standard Code of Practice relating to such a product, where the EC marking relates to the same characteristic and specific purpose as the Certificate, Standard or Code of Practice.

(8) Where for the purposes of these regulations testing is carried out, it shall be carried out by an appropriate organisation offering suitable and satisfactory evidence of technical and professional competence and independence and such condition shall be satisfied where the testing organisation is accredited in an EEA State in accordance with the relevant parts of the EN 45000 series of standards for the tests carried out.

(9) Any note in a Table or Schedule shall be treated for all purposes as a substantive provision.

(10) Any reference in these regulations, other than in paragraphs (6)(a) to (d), to a publication shall be construed as follows—

(a) in regulation B3 and in any other case where no date is included in the reference, the reference is to the edition thereof current at 28 February 1994 together with any amendments, supplements or addenda thereto published at that date;

(b) in any case where a date is included in the reference, the reference is to the edition of that date, together with such amendments, as are mentioned in Schedule 3; and

(c) any reference to any publication is a reference to so much only thereof as is relevant in the context in which such publication is quoted.

(11) The abbreviations and symbols listed in the following Table are used in these regulations—

Abbreviation or symbol	Definition
BS	British Standard
CP	British Standard Code of Practice
°	degree (angular measure)
°C	degree Celsius
kW	kilowatt
m	metre
m^2	square metre
m^3	cubic metre
mm	millimetre
mm^2	square millimetre
W	watt

A3 Deemed-to-satisfy provisions

Where any provision (in these regulations called a deemed-to-satisfy provision) states that the use of a particular material, method of construction or specification shall be deemed to satisfy the requirement of any regulation or part thereof, that provision shall not be construed so as to require any person necessarily to use such material, method of construction or specification.

A4 Transitional provisions

(1) In this regulation—

WORK means the erection of a building, the alteration or extension of a building, the execution of works, the installation of a fitting or the making of a material change of use (within the meaning of the Building Regulations (Northern Ireland) 1990(**a**)).

(2) These regulations shall not apply to—

(a) plans which were deposited with the district council before 28 November 1994;

(b) work carried out in accordance with such plans with or without any departure or deviation from those plans; and

(c) work completed before that date.

(3) The Building Regulations (Northern Ireland) 1973(**b**) shall continue to apply to—

(a) plans deposited in accordance with those regulations before 1 October 1977;

(b) work carried out in accordance with such plans with or without any departure or deviation from those plans; and

(c) work completed on or after 1 October 1973 but before 1 October 1977, other than work to which building bye-laws continue to apply in accordance with paragraph 2 of Schedule 2 to the Building Regulations (Northern Ireland) Order 1979.

(4) The Building Regulations (Northern Ireland) 1977(**c**) shall continue to apply to—

(a) plans deposited in accordance with those regulations before 1 June 1990;

(b) work carried out in accordance with such plans with or without any departure or deviation from those plans; and

---

(**a**) SR 1990 No 59 (NI) as amended by SR 1991 No 169 and SR 1993 No 84
(**b**) SR & O (NI) 1973 No 105 as amended by SR & O (NI) 1973 No 506 and SR 1975 No 112
(**c**) SR 1977 No 149 as amended by SR 1979 No 79, SR 1980 No 86; SR 1980 No 332; SR 1982 No 81; SR 1984 No 295; SR 1984 No 343 and SR 1987 No 268

(c) work completed on or after 1 October 1977 but before 1 June 1990, other than work to which building bye-laws continue to apply in accordance with paragraph 2 of Schedule 2 to the Building Regulations (Northern Ireland) Order 1979 and work to which the Building Regulations (Northern Ireland) 1973 continue to apply by virtue of paragraph (3).

(5) The Building Regulations (Northern Ireland) 1990 shall continue to apply to—

(a) plans deposited in accordance with those regulations before 28 November 1994;

(b) work carried out in accordance with such plans with or without any departure or deviation from those plans; and

(c) work completed on or after 1 June 1990 but before 28 November 1994, other than work to which building bye-laws continue to apply in accordance with paragraph 2 of Schedule 2 to the Building Regulations (Northern Ireland) Order 1979 and work to which the Building Regulations (Northern Ireland) 1973 and 1977 continue to apply by virtue of paragraphs (3) and (4).

A5 Exemptions

(1) Subject to paragraph (3), these regulations shall not apply to—

(a) building work in connection with any buildings belonging to any statutory undertaking and held or used by them for the purposes of their undertaking provided that this exemption shall not extend to dwellings or to buildings used as offices, shops, showrooms or passenger stations for air, road, rail or sea travel;

(b) the erection of any wholly exempted building (including the provision of any service or fitting solely in connection therewith); and

(c) the alteration or extension of or the provision of any service or fitting solely in connection with, a wholly exempted building, if after the carrying out of that work the building remains a wholly exempted building.

(2) Subject to paragraph (3), in the application of these regulations to—

(i) the erection of a partially exempted building;

(ii) the provision of a service or fitting in connection with a partially exempted building; or

(iii) the alteration or extension of a partially exempted building in such a way that it will remain a partially exempted building, as so altered or extended, it shall only be necessary to comply with the provisions of these regulations which are specified in paragraph 2 of Part A of Schedule 1.

(3) The building work in paragraphs (1) and (2) shall not create a ncw or greater contravention of any relevant requirement of these regulations in any part of a building or in any other building to which these regulations apply.

(4) In determining for the purposes of paragraph (3) whether any building work would cause a new or greater contravention of any of these regulations, sub-paragraphs (a) and (b) of regulation A7(3) shall apply.

(5) For the purposes of paragraph (3) and Schedule 1 —

(a) a building shall not be regarded as attached to another building solely by virtue of it being attached to a fence, garden wall or similar structure; and

(b) BUILDING TO WHICH THESE REGULATIONS APPLY means a building which, if it were being newly erected, would be subject to the control of any regulation in Parts C to K, regulations L2(2) and (3) and L7 and Parts R and V.

A6 Application to erection of buildings

Subject to the provisions of regulation A5, the following provisions, that is to say, Parts A to K, regulations L2(2) and (3) and L7 and Parts R and V shall apply to the erection of a building.

A7 Application to alterations and extensions

(1) Subject to the provisions of paragraph (4) and regulation A5, the following provisions, that is to say, Parts A to K, regulations L2(2) and (3) and L7 and Parts R and V shall apply to—

(a) a structural alteration or extension of an existing building; and

(b) the existing building as affected by that alteration or extension to the extent (subject to the provisions of regulation A9) of prohibiting any alteration or extension which would cause a new or greater contravention of any regulation.

(2) In applying the regulations under paragraph (1)(a), the alteration or extension shall be treated as if it were part of a building being newly erected identical to and to be used for the same purposes as the building as altered or extended.

(3) In determining for the purposes of paragraph (1)(b) whether the alteration or extension would cause a new or greater contravention of any regulation, the following provisions shall apply—

(a) the regulations shall be applied in each of the following ways—

     (i)   to the building as altered or extended treated as if it were being newly erected in its proposed form for the purposes for which it will be used when altered or extended; and

     (ii)   to the existing building treated as if it were being newly erected in its existing form but for the purposes for which it will be used when altered or extended; and

  (b) the alteration or extension shall be regarded as being such as would cause a new or greater contravention if (when the regulations are applied as directed in sub-paragraph (a)) the building as altered or extended—

     (i)   contravenes any regulation which does not apply to the existing building;

     (ii)   contravenes any regulation which is satisfied by the existing building; or

     (iii)   contravenes to a greater extent any regulation which is contravened by the existing building.

(4)   Part R shall only apply to—

  (a) the ground storey of an extension to a building to which Part R did not apply when built if—

     (i)   the area of the ground storey of the extension exceeds 10% of the area of the ground storey of the building to be extended and is greater than 200 m^2;

     (ii)   the extension incorporates an external entrance; or

     (iii) there is access for disabled people to and within the ground storey of the building to be extended;

  (b) the alteration or extension of any storey to which Part R applied when that storey was erected;

  (c) the vertical extension of a building to the uppermost storey of which Part R applied when that storey was erected; and

  (d) the provision or alteration of a facility provided for disabled people.

A8 Application to services and fittings

Subject to any express provision to the contrary and the provisions of regulation A5—

Part A (Interpretation and general)
In Part B (Materials and workmanship) regulation B2
Part E (Fire safety)
In Part F (Conservation of fuel and power) regulations F4 and F6
Part K (Ventilation)
In Part L (Heat-producing appliances and liquefied petroleum gas installations) regulations L2(1), L4 and L5
Part N (Drainage)
Part P (Sanitary appliances and unvented hot water storage systems)

shall apply to the provision of any service and fitting (whether by way of new work, alteration or replacement) to which any of those Parts respectively relate.

A9   Application to material change of use

(1)   For the purposes of these regulations a change in the purposes for which or the circumstances in which a building, or part of a building, is used shall only be regarded as a material change of use if after that change any one of the following cases applies—

Case I –   the building is used as a dwellinghouse, where previously it was not.

Case II –   the building contains a flat or maisonette, where previously it did not.

Case III –   the building is used as —

(a) a hotel or boarding house, where previously it was not;

(b) an institution, where previously it was not;

(c) a public building, where previously it was not;

(d) a shop, where previously it was not;

(e) an office, where previously it was not; or

(f) a store, where previously it was not.

Case IV – the building, by virtue of the change of use, is not a wholly exempted or a partially exempted building where previously it was.

(2)   Where there is a material change of use to the whole or part of a building the provisions of the regulations set out in the Table to this regulation shall apply.

Table to Regulation A9

Application to material change of use

Parts		Cases			
		I	II	III#	IV
A	Interpretation and general	*	*	*	*
B	Materials and workmanship	–	–	–	*
C	Preparation of site and resistance to moisture	*[1]	*[1]	*[1]	*[1]
D	Structure	*[2]	*[2]	*[2]	*
E	Fire safety	*[3]	*[3]	*[3]	*[3]
F	Conservation of fuel and power	–	–	–	–
G	Sound insulation of dwellings	*	*	–	*
H	Stairs, ramps and guarding	–	–	–	*

Table to Regulation A9 – continued

Parts		I	II	III#	IV
				Cases	
J	Solid waste in buildings	*	*	*	*
K	Ventilation	*	*	*	*
L	Heat-producing appliances and LPG installations	$*^4$	$*^4$	$*^4$	$*^4$
N	Drainage	–	–	–	–
P	Sanitary appliances and unvented hot water storage systems	$*^5$	$*^5$	$*^5$	$*^5$
R	Access and facilities for disabled people	–	–	–	–
V	Glazing	*	*	–	–

Notes to Table

\# Only Parts A, D and E shall apply to Case III(d) to (f) and, in the application of Parts D and E, only insofar as indicated by Notes 2 and 3 respectively.

* Denotes Parts which apply.

– Denotes Parts which do not apply.

1 All regulations except C2 and C4.

2 Part D shall apply to those parts of the building affected by any increase in imposed loading resulting from the change of use.

3 In the application of Part E the requirements of regulation E8 shall only apply, in relation to external walls, when the height of a building exceeds 20 m (such height shall be measured from the mean level of the ground adjoining the outside of the external walls of the building to the level of half the vertical height of the roof of the building, or to the top of the walls or of the parapet, if any, whichever is the higher).

4 Regulations L2(2) and (3) only.

5 All regulations except P5.

(3) Where a material change of use neither involves nor is accompanied by an alteration or extension, the provisions referred to in the Table to this regulation shall apply to the building or part of the building in which the change of use occurs as if it were a new building identical to the building as it exists and to be used for the same purpose or purposes as the building will have after the change of use.

(4) Where a material change of use involves or is accompanied by an alteration or extension—

(a) the provisions referred to in the Table to this regulation (other than regulation A8) shall apply to the building or part of the building in which the change of use occurs as if it were part of a new building identical to the building as altered or extended and to be used for the same purpose or purposes as that building will have after the change of use; and

(b) the application of regulation A7 by paragraph (2) shall apply any requirements of that regulation which are additional to those directly applied by the Table to this regulation.

(5) Where a change of use will result in a wholly exempted or a partially exempted building being put to a use as described in Cases I, II or III the provisions of those regulations applicable to Case IV shall apply in precedence to those of Cases I, II or III.

A10 Giving of notices and deposit of plans

(1) Subject to the provisions of paragraphs (2), (3) and (5), any person who intends to carry out any building work to or make any material change of use of a building shall, if any provisions of these regulations apply to such work or such change of use, give notices and deposit plans, sections, specifications and written particulars in accordance with the relevant rules of Schedule 2.

(2) The provisions of paragraph (1) shall not apply to—

(a) the provision of a heat-producing appliance to which Part L relates, by way of replacement of an existing heat-producing appliance, if compliance with the relevant regulations in that Part does not require the carrying out of any structural alteration;

(b) the provision of a fitting to which Part N or P (except regulation P5) relates, by way of replacement of an existing fitting, if compliance with the relevant regulations in that Part does not require the carrying out of any structural alteration; and

(c) the replacement of windows.

(3) The provisions of paragraph (1) where they relate to the requirements of regulation F6 shall not apply where the work involves only the extension of an existing system and does not involve the carrying out of any structural alteration.

(4) In paragraph (2)(a) heat-producing appliance has the same meaning as in Part L.

(5) Notwithstanding that the replacement of windows does not require the giving of notices or deposit of plans and other particulars, the work of replacement shall in all respects meet any relevant requirements of these regulations.

A11 Notice of commencement and completion of certain stages of work

(1) In this regulation—

    (a) BUILDER means any person carrying out or intending to carry out any building work to which any of these regulations apply; and

    (b) in the calculation of a period of notice, DAY means any period of 24 hours commencing at midnight on the day on which the notice is given and excludes any Saturday, Sunday or public holiday.

(2) Subject to the provisions of paragraph (6), a builder shall furnish the district council with—

    (a) not less than 2 days notice in writing of the date and time at which the operation will be commenced;

    (b) not less than 2 days notice in writing before the covering up of any excavation for a foundation, any foundation, any damp-proof course or any concrete or other material laid over a site;

    (c) not less than 2 days notice in writing before any drain or private sewer to which these regulations apply will be haunched or covered in any way; and

    (d) notice in writing not more than 5 days after the work of laying such drain or private sewer has been carried out, including any necessary work of haunching or surrounding the drain or private sewer with concrete and backfilling the trench.

(3) If the builder neglects or refuses to give any such notice, he or any person appearing to the district council to have control over the work or the building as the case may be shall comply with any notice in writing from the district council requiring him within a reasonable time to cut into, lay open or pull down so much of the building, services or fittings as prevents the district council from ascertaining whether any of these regulations have been contravened.

(4) If the builder, in accordance with any notice in writing received from the district council which specifies the manner in which any building or services or fittings contravenes the requirements of these regulations, has altered or added to the building, services or fittings so as to secure compliance with these regulations, he shall, within a reasonable time after the completion of such alteration or addition, give notice in writing to the district council of its completion.

(5) Subject to the provisions of paragraph (6), the builder shall give to the district council notice in writing of—

    (a) the erection of a building, not more than 5 days after completion, or (if a building or part of a building is occupied before completion) not less than 5 days before occupation as well as not more than 5 days after completion;

(b) any alteration or extension of a building, not more than 5 days after completion; and

(c) the provision of any service or fitting in connection with a building, not more than 5 days after completion.

(6) The requirements of this regulation shall not apply to the provision of any fitting if the giving of notices and the deposit of plans, sections, specifications and written particulars are not required under the provisions of regulation A10.

A12 Completion certificates

(1) Where in relation to any building work, carried out in relation to a building or part of a building, a district council has been able to ascertain after taking all reasonable steps in that behalf, that relevant requirements of these regulations have been satisfied, it may issue a certificate (in this regulation referred to as a 'completion certificate') specifying the requirements so satisfied.

(2) Subject to and in accordance with paragraph (1) and without prejudice to the generality of that paragraph, a district council shall issue a completion certificate in relation to any building work where—

(a) it has approved plans for the building work; and

(b) it has—

    (i)   been requested to do so; or

    (ii) been notified (in accordance with paragraph 5 of Rule A of Schedule 2) that the building work is in relation to a building which is or is intended to be put to a use which is a designated use for the purposes of the Fire Services (Northern Ireland) Order 1984 **(a)** and been requested to do so in respect of that notification.

(3) Without prejudice to paragraph (2), a district council may in accordance with paragraph (1) issue a completion certificate in such other circumstances as it may think fit and proper.

(4) For the purposes of paragraph (1) the relevant requirements of these regulations are—

(a) in relation to building work generally – any requirement of these regulations which apply in relation to that building work; and

(b) in relation to any building work mentioned in paragraph (2) (b) (ii) – the requirements of Part E.

(a) SI 1984 No 1821 (NI 11)

(5)   Any person having an interest to do so may apply for a completion certificate.

(6)   A completion certificate issued in accordance with this regulation shall be evidence (but not conclusive evidence) that the relevant requirements specified in the certificate have been complied with.

A13 Testing of drains and private sewers

An authorised officer of the district council shall be permitted to make such tests of any drain or private sewer as may be necessary to establish compliance with any of the provisions of Part N.

A14 Sampling of materials

An authorised officer of the district council shall at all reasonable times be permitted to take such samples of the materials used or to be used in the erection, alteration or extension of a building, or the provision of services or fittings, as may be necessary to enable the district council to ascertain whether such materials comply with the provisions of these regulations.

A15 Exercise of power of dispensation or relaxation

(1)   Subject to paragraph (2), the power under Article 15(1) of the Building Regulations (Northern Ireland) Order 1979 to dispense with or relax any requirement of building regulations shall, in accordance with Article 15(2) of the said Order, be exercisable by the district council in relation to any requirement of these regulations other than those in—

Part A (Interpretation and general)

Part D (Structure).

(2)   Paragraph (1) shall not apply to any application made by a district council.

A16 Application for dispensation or relaxation

(1)   Any application for a direction dispensing with or relaxing any requirement of these regulations shall be submitted in duplicate.

(2)   Before giving a direction the Department or, as the case may be, the district council may if it thinks fit send—

(a) to the applicant, a copy of its draft direction; and

(b) to any other person or body appearing to it to be interested, a copy of the application and of its draft direction,

inviting comment on the draft direction, and it shall take into account any comments received before making the direction final.

(3) Before giving a direction the Department or, as the case may be, the district council may if it thinks fit afford to the applicant or any other person appearing to it to be interested, an opportunity of appearing before and being heard by a person appointed by the Department or, as the case may be, the district council for that purpose.

(4) After giving a direction the Department or, as the case may be, the district council shall notify the applicant and any other person who was sent a copy of the draft direction under paragraph (2), of the direction and its reasons therefor.

A17 Appeals and prescribed periods

(1) Where the applicant has a right of appeal to the Department under Articles 16, 17 or 18B of the Building Regulations (Northern Ireland) Order 1979 **(a)** against a decision of a district council the notification of that decision to the applicant shall indicate—

(a) that there is a right of appeal;

(b) where the decision relates to a contravention notice, that in addition to a right of appeal against the service of the notice there is also a right to obtain a report under Article 18A of the Building Regulations (Northern Ireland) Order 1979 in respect of the notice and the periods within which he may notify the district council of his intention to obtain such a report and (where he has obtained it) submit it to the council;

(c) the prescribed period within which the appeal may be made; and

(d) the requirements of paragraph (2).

(2) An appeal to the Department shall set out the grounds of appeal and a copy shall be sent to the district council.

(3) The district council on receiving the copy of the appeal shall at once transmit to the Department a copy of the application and a copy of all documents furnished by the applicant for the purposes of his application.

(4) The district council shall at the same time give to the Department in writing any representations which it desires to make as regards the appeal and shall send a copy to the appellant.

(5) The prescribed period for the purposes of Article 16(1) of the Building Regulations (Northern Ireland) Order 1979 (appeal against refusal by a

---

(a) SI 1979 No 1709 (NI 16), Article 18B was inserted by SI 1990 No 1510 (NI 14)

district council to dispense with or relax regulations or against conditions attaching to dispensation or relaxation) shall be 56 days.

(6) The prescribed period for the purposes of Article 16(2) of the Building Regulations (Northern Ireland) Order 1979 (period for consideration of application for relaxation by a district council) shall be 56 days.

(7) The prescribed period for the purposes of Article 17(1) of the Building Regulations (Northern Ireland) Order 1979 (appeal against rejection of plans by a district council) shall be 56 days.

(8) The prescribed period for the purposes of Article 17(2) of the Building Regulations (Northern Ireland) Order 1979 (period after which an applicant may assume plans to be rejected) shall be 56 days.

A18 Revocations

Subject to the provisions of regulation A4 the regulations specified in the Table to this regulation are hereby revoked.

Table to Regulation A18

Regulations revoked (1)	References (2)
The Building Regulations (Northern Ireland) 1990	SR 1990 No 59
The Building (Amendment) Regulations (Northern Ireland) 1991	SR 1991 No 169
The Building (Amendment) Regulations (Northern Ireland) 1993	SR 1993 No 84

Part B

Materials and workmanship

B1 Interpretation

In this Part—

HARMFUL SUBSTANCE includes fumes and vapours;

MATERIALS includes any fittings, components or other manufactured products; and

RELEVANT WORK means—

(a) the erection of a building;

(b) the structural alteration or extension of a building;

(c) the provision of any service or fitting; or

(d) the backfilling of any excavation carried out in connection with (a), (b) or (c).

B2 Fitness of materials and workmanship

In any relevant work—

(a) the materials used shall—

    (i) be of a suitable nature and quality in relation to the purposes for and the conditions in which they are used;

    (ii) be adequately mixed and prepared;

    (iii) be applied, used or fixed so as adequately to perform the functions for which they are designed; and

    (iv) not continue to emit any harmful substance longer than is reasonable in the circumstances; and

(b) the standards of materials and workmanship need be no more than are necessary to secure the health and safety of people in or about the building and, where appropriate, the convenience of disabled people and the conservation of fuel and power.

B3 Deemed-to-satisfy provisions regarding the fitness of materials and workmanship

Subject to regulations B4 and B5, the use of any material or any method of mixing or preparing materials or of applying, using or fixing materials, which conforms with a British Standard or a British Standard Code of Practice prescribing the quality or classification of material or standards of workmanship, shall be deemed to be a sufficient compliance with the requirements of regulation B2 if the use of that material or method is appropriate to the purpose for and conditions in which it is used.

B4 Suitability of certain materials

(1) In determining whether a material is of a suitable nature and quality for use as the weather-resisting part of an external wall or roof no account shall be taken of that material being either—

(a) painted; or

(b) coated, surfaced or rendered with any other material which, when so used, does not in itself constitute effective resistance against weather.

(2) The preservative treatment for timber against decay shall be carried out in accordance with BS 5589: 1989: Section 2 for performance category B.

(3) Any material which depends on periodic maintenance, replacement or renewal for its suitability shall be readily accessible or positioned so that such maintenance, replacement or renewal is practicable.

B5 Urea formaldehyde foam

(1) Subject to paragraph (2), in situ foamed urea formaldehyde shall not be used in the erection, structural alteration or extension of a building.

(2) In situ foamed urea formaldehyde may be used for filling the cavity of a cavity wall having an inner leaf constructed of bricks or blocks, provided that it is manufactured, prepared and installed in accordance with BS 5617: 1985 and BS 5618: 1985.

Part C

Preparation of site and resistance to moisture

C1 Application and interpretation

(1) Regulation C2(2) shall not apply in relation to an existing dwelling or part of an existing dwelling—

(a) which is altered; or

(b) which is extended by less than 30 m²,

if measures to prevent or limit the ingress of radon are not already incorporated in that dwelling.

(2) Regulation C5 in respect of resistance to ground moisture of floors and walls, and weather resistance of walls shall not apply where the building is intended to be used wholly for—

(a) storing goods, provided that any person who is habitually employed in the building is engaged only in storing, caring for or removing the goods; or

(b) a purpose such that compliance with regulation C5 would not serve to increase protection to the health or safety of any person habitually employed in the building.

(3) Regulation C7 applies only to a dwelling.

(4) In this Part—

DANGEROUS AND HARMFUL SUBSTANCES includes any substance which is or could become corrosive, explosive, inflammable, radioactive or toxic and includes deposits of faecal or animal matter;

FLOOR includes any base or structure between the surface of the ground, or the surface of any hardcore laid upon the ground, and the upper surface of the floor;

MOISTURE includes water vapour as well as liquid water; and

WALL includes piers, chimneys, columns and parapets which form part of the wall.

C2   Preparation of site and resistance to dangerous and harmful substances

(1)   The site of a building and the ground adjacent to it shall be prepared and treated, and measures shall be taken, so as to prevent, as far as reasonably practicable, any harmful effect on the building or the health or safety of the occupants caused by—

(a) vegetable soil; and

(b) dangerous or harmful substances.

(2)   Without prejudice to the generality of paragraph (1) measures shall be taken to prevent or limit the ingress of radon from the ground into any dwelling situated in any zone marked on the map set out in Schedule 4.

C3   *Deemed-to-satisfy provisions relating to radon*

(1)   The requirements of regulation C2(2) shall be deemed to be satisfied in relation to any work described in columns (1) and (2) of the Table to this regulation which is situated in—

(a) zone A, if that work complies with the requirements specified opposite thereto in column (3);

(b) zone B, if that work complies with the requirements specified opposite thereto in column (4); and

(c) zone C, if that work complies with the requirements specified opposite thereto in column (5).

(2)   In this regulation any reference to a particular zone shall be construed as a reference to the zone which is marked as such on the map set out in Schedule 4.

Table to Regulation C3

Measures to prevent or limit the ingress of radon

Description of work		Zone A	Zone B	Zone C
(1)	*(2)*	*(3)*	*(4)*	*(5)*
1. *The erection of any dwelling and the extension by more than 30m² of a dwelling which does not already incorporate measures to prevent or limit the ingress of radon from the ground*	(a) *Where a floor next to the ground is above a void or where there is a void behind a wall*	*The void shall be adequately ventilated*	*The void shall be adequately ventilated and a radon proof membrane shall be incorporated in the construction*	*The void shall be adequately ventilated and a radon proof membrane shall be incorporated in the construction*
	(b) *In any other case*	*A radon proof membrane shall be incorporated in the construction*	*A radon proof membrane shall be incorporated in the construction and a sump and stub-duct shall be installed*	*A radon proof barrier shall be incorporated in the construction and a sump and stub-duct shall be installed*
2. *The alteration or extension of a dwelling which already incorporates measures to prevent or limit the ingress of radon from the ground*		*The same measures as are incorporated in the existing building shall be maintained or extended, as the case may be, so as to apply throughout the dwelling as altered or extended*		

C4 Subsoil drainage

The site of a building and the ground adjacent to it shall be drained as far as reasonably practicable, or the building otherwise protected so as to prevent any harmful effect on the building or the health of the occupants caused by—

(a) ground water; and

(b) existing subsoil drainage.

C5 Resistance to ground moisture and weather

Every wall, floor and roof shall be constructed so as to prevent any harmful effect on the building or the health of the occupants caused by the passage of moisture to any part of the building from—

(a) the ground; and

(b) the weather.

C6 *Deemed-to-satisfy provision for resistance to ground moisture and weather*

The requirements of regulation C5 in respect of walls and floors shall be deemed to be satisfied if they are constructed in accordance with DOE(NI) Technical Booklet C: 1994.

C7 Condensation

A building to which this regulation applies shall be designed and constructed so as to prevent, as far as reasonably practicable, any harmful effect on the building from moisture in the form of interstitial condensation.

C8 *Deemed-to-satisfy provision for condensation*

The requirements of regulation C7 shall be deemed to be satisfied if the building is designed and constructed in accordance with BS 5250: 1989, Clauses 9.1 to 9.5.

Part D

Structure

D1 Loading

The loads to which a building will be subjected shall be calculated in accordance with, in the case of—

(a) dead and imposed loads (excluding imposed roof loads) – BS 6399: Part 1: 1984;

(b) imposed roof loads – BS 6399: Part 3: 1988; and

(c) wind loads – CP 3: Chapter V: Part 2: 1972 (in no case shall S3 be taken as less than 1):

Provided that—

(i) the actual load is used, where the actual load to which a building is to be subjected is likely to exceed the load so calculated; and

(ii) loads used allow for possible dynamic, concentrated and peak load effects which may occur.

D2 Stability

The building shall be designed and constructed so that the combined dead, imposed and wind loads are sustained and transmitted to the ground, taking into account the nature of the ground—

(a) safely; and

(b) without impairing the safety of any part of another building.

D3 *Deemed-to-satisfy provisions for stability*

The requirements of regulation D2 shall be deemed to be satisfied if the design and construction of the work is carried out in accordance with the relevant recommendations of the following documents, that is to say, in the case of—

(a) foundations—

    (i)   BS 8004: 1986; or

    (ii)   DOE(NI) Technical Booklet D: 1994: Sections 1 and 5 (for houses and small buildings);

(b) *structural work of reinforced, prestressed or plain concrete—*
    BS 8110: Part 1: 1985, BS 8110: Part 2: 1985 and
    BS 8110: Part 3: 1985;

(c) *structural work of steel—*

    (i) *BS 449: Part 2: 1969;*

    (ii) *BS 5950: Part 1: 1990, BS 5950: Part 2: 1992 and BS 5950: Part 5: 1987; or*

    (iii) *BS 5950: Part 4: 1982 and 1994;*

(d) *structural work of composite steel and concrete construction—*
    BS 5950: Part 3: Section 3.1: 1990;

(e) *structural work of aluminium—*

    (i) *CP118: 1969 using one of the principal or supplementary aluminium alloys designated in Section 1.1 of that Code; and for the purpose of Section 5.3 of that Code, the structure shall be classified as a safe-life structure; or*

    (ii) *BS 8118: Part 1: 1991 and BS 8118: Part 2: 1991;*

(f) *structural work of masonry—*

    (i) *BS 5628: Part 1: 1992, BS 5628: Part 2: 1985 and BS 5628: Part 3: 1985; or*

    (ii) *DOE(NI) Technical Booklet D: 1994: Sections 1, 3 and 4 (for residential buildings of not more than 3 storeys, small single storey non-residential buildings and small buildings forming annexes to residential buildings (including garages and outbuildings)); and*

(g) *structural work of timber—*

    (i) *BS 5268: Part 2: 1991 and BS 5268: Part 3: 1985; or*

    (ii) *DOE(NI) Technical Booklet D: 1994: Sections 1 and 2 (for single family houses of not more than 3 storeys).*

D4   Disproportionate collapse

(1) A building to which this paragraph applies shall be designed and constructed so that in the event of damage occurring to any part of the building, the extent of any resultant collapse will not be disproportionate to the cause of the damage.

(2) Paragraph (1) applies to a building having 5 or more storeys, counting each basement level as one storey but discounting a storey within a roof space where the slope of the roof does not exceed 70° to the horizontal.

D5   *Deemed-to-satisfy provisions for disproportionate collapse*

The requirements of regulation D4 shall be deemed to be satisfied in relation to any building if the design and construction of the work on that building is in accordance with—

(a) the relevant recommendations of the following documents (taking account of the recommendations on ties and on the effect of misuse or accident), that is to say, in the case of—

   (i)   structural work of reinforced, prestressed or plain concrete—

   BS 8110: Parts 1 and 2: 1985;

   (ii)   structural work of steel—

   BS 5950: Part 1: 1990 (the accidental loading referred to in clause 2.4.5.5 shall be chosen having particular regard to the importance of the key elements and the consequences of failure, and the key element shall always be capable of withstanding a load of at least 34 kN/m² applied from any direction); and

   (iii) structural work of masonry—

   BS 5628: Part 1: 1992; and

(b) the procedures contained in DOE(NI) Technical Booklet D: 1994: Section 6.

Part E

Fire safety

E1 Application and interpretation

(1) Regulations E2 and E6(3) shall not apply to a prison within the meaning of the Prisons Act (Northern Ireland) 1953(a), or any other place of lawful detention.

(2) In this Part—

ASSEMBLY BUILDING includes places of entertainment or recreation; conference, exhibition, and leisure centres; museums and art galleries; law courts; churches and other buildings for worship; libraries open to the public; health centres and surgeries; passenger stations for air, rail, road and sea travel; and public toilets;

DWELLING means a self-contained unit of residential accommodation occupied (whether or not as a sole or main residence)—

(a) by a single person or by people living together as a family; or

(b) by not more than 6 people living together as a single household, including a household where care is provided for residents;

DWELLINGHOUSE means a dwelling on one or more storeys which is detached or forms part of a building from all other parts of which it is divided only vertically;

FLAT means a dwelling on one storey forming part of a building from some other part of which it is divided horizontally;

HOUSE IN MULTIPLE OCCUPATION means a building, or part of a building, occupied by people who do not form a single household and containing units of residential accommodation which are not self-contained;

INTERNAL LININGS means the materials lining any partition, wall, ceiling or other internal structure;

(a) 1953 c.18 (N.I.)

MAISONETTE means a dwelling on more than one storey forming part of a building from some other part of which it is divided horizontally;

MEANS OF ESCAPE means structural means whereby, in the event of a fire, a safe route or routes is or are provided for people to travel from any point in a building to a place of safety;

OFFICE includes premises used for the purposes of administration; clerical work; handling money; and communications;

PLACE OF SAFETY means a place, outside the building, in which persons are in no danger from fire;

RESIDENTIAL HEALTH CARE BUILDING includes nursing homes; homes for old people, children, mentally ill and the mentally or physically handicapped;

SHOPPING COMPLEX means a shopping complex that includes a covered mall in which—

(a) more than 15 m of the length of the mall section is covered by a bridge or roof; or

(b) at least one-quarter of its plan area is obscured by a roof or by floors, bridges, galleries or canopies, unless there is a continuous open slot above the mall section in which case more than one-half of its plan area is obscured; and

SPECTATOR ACCOMMODATION means covered seating accommodation at sports grounds.

E2   Means of escape

A building shall be so designed and constructed that in the event of a fire there is—

(a) where appropriate, adequate means of automatic detection;

(b) adequate means of giving warning; and

(c) adequate means of escape, which can be safely and effectively used at all material times.

E3   *Deemed-to-satisfy provisions for means of escape*

The requirements of regulation E2 shall be deemed to be satisfied if the means of automatic detection, warning and the means of escape are in accordance with the relevant requirements of the following documents, that is to say, in the case of—

(a) a dwellinghouse –
   DOE(NI) Technical Booklet E: 1994: Sections 1 and 6;

(b) a flat or maisonette –
   BS 5588 Part 1: 1990;

(c) *a hospital—*

   (i)   *Health Technical Memorandum 81 published by Department of Health and Social Security 1989;*

   (ii) *Nucleus Fire Precautions Recommendations published by Department of Health: 1989; or*

   (iii) *Draft Guide to Fire Precautions in Hospitals published by Home Office: 1982;*

(d) *a residential health care building—*

   (i)   *Health Technical Memorandum 88 published by Department of Health and Social Security: 1986; or*

   (ii) *Draft Guide to Fire Precautions in Existing Residential Care Premises published by Home Office: 1983;*

(e) *a house in multiple occupation—*

    Section 5 of DOE Circular 12/92 published by Department of the Environment: 1992;

(f) *a hotel or boarding house—*

    Chapters 13 and 14 of the Guide to Fire Precautions in Premises Used as Hotels and Boarding Houses Which Require a Fire Certificate published by Home Office: 1991;

(g) *an office—*

   (i)   *DOE(NI) Technical Booklet E: 1994: Sections 1 and 6; and BS 5588: Part 8: 1988; or*

   (ii) *BS 5588: Part 3: 1983 and BS 5588: Part 8: 1988;*

(h) *a shop—*

   (i)   *DOE(NI) Technical Booklet E: 1994: Sections 1 and 6; and BS 5588: Part 8: 1988; or*

   (ii) *BS 5588: Part 2: 1985 and BS 5588: Part 8: 1988;*

(i) *a shopping complex—*

    BS 5588: Part 10: 1991 and BS 5588: Part 8: 1988;

(j) *an assembly building (other than spectator accomodation at sports grounds)—*

   (i)   *DOE(NI) Technical Booklet E: 1994: Sections 1 and 6; and BS 5588: Part 8: 1988; or*

   (ii) *BS 5588: Part 6: 1991 and BS 5588: Part 8: 1988;*

(k) *an educational building—*

    Building Bulletin 7 published by Department of Education and Science: 1988; and BS 5588: Part 8: 1988;

(l) *spectator accommodation at a sports ground—*

    Guide to Safety at Sports Grounds published by Home Office: 1990; or

(m) *any other non-residential building—*

> *DOE(NI) Technical Booklet E: 1994: Sections 1 and 6; and BS 5588: Part 8: 1988.*

E4 Internal fire spread – Linings

To inhibit the spread of fire within a building the internal linings shall—

(a) offer adequate resistance to the spread of flame over their surfaces; and

(b) where they are located in a circulation space, have a low rate of heat release when ignited.

E5 *Deemed-to-satisfy provision for internal fire spread – Linings*

The requirements of regulation E4 shall be deemed to be satisfied if the internal linings are designed and constructed in accordance with DOE(NI) Technical Booklet E: 1994: Sections 2 and 6.

E6 Internal fire spread – Structure

(1) A building shall be so designed and constructed that, in the event of a fire, its stability will be retained for a reasonable period.

(2) A wall common to two or more buildings shall be so designed and constructed that it provides adequate resistance to the spread of fire between those buildings and for the purposes of this paragraph a dwellinghouse in a terrace and a semi-detached dwellinghouse shall be considered as a separate building.

(3) To inhibit the spread of fire within it, a building shall be adequately sub-divided with fire-resisting construction.

(4) A building shall be so designed and constructed that the spread of fire (and in particular smoke) within concealed spaces in its structure and fabric is adequately inhibited.

E7 *Deemed-to-satisfy provisions for internal fire spread – Structure*

The requirements of regulation E6 shall be deemed to be satisfied if the building is designed and constructed in accordance with, in the case of—

(a) *a shopping complex –*
> *the relevant recommendations of BS 5588: Part 10: 1991: Sections 5 and 6; or*

(b) *any other building –*
> *DOE(NI) Technical Booklet E: 1994: Sections 3 and 6.*

E8 External fire spread

The external walls and roof of a building shall be so designed and constructed that they afford adequate resistance to the spread of fire over them , and from one building to another, having regard to—

(a) in the case of an external wall – the use, position and height of the building; and

(b) in the case of a roof – the use and position of the building.

E9　Deemed-to-satisfy provision for external fire spread

The requirements of regulation E8 shall be deemed to be satisfied if the building is designed and constructed in accordance with DOE(NI) Technical Booklet E: 1994: Sections 4 and 6.

E10　Facilities and access for the Fire Brigade

(1) A building shall be designed and constructed with such reasonable facilities as are necessary to assist the Fire Brigade in ensuring the safety of people in and about the building in the event of a fire.

(2) Reasonable provisions shall be made within the boundary of the premises for access to the building by fire brigade appliances for the purpose of paragraph (1).

E11　Deemed-to-satisfy provision for facilities and access for the Fire Brigade

The requirements of regulation E10 shall be deemed to be satisfied if the building and access thereto are designed and constructed in accordance with DOE(NI) Technical Booklet E: 1994: Sections 5 and 6.

Part F

Conservation of fuel and power

F1   Application and interpretation

(1)   Subject to paragraph (2) this Part shall apply to any building and, where a building contains one or more dwellings, to each such dwelling separately.

(2)   Regulation F2 shall not apply to—

    (a) an external wall, floor or roof of any part of a dwelling which consists of—

        (i)   a shed or store entered solely from outside; or

        (ii)   a boathouse, conservatory, garage or porch;

    (b) a building, other than a dwelling, which has a floor area not exceeding 30 m²; and

    (c) a building or part of a building, other than a dwelling, which—

        (i)   in the case of a building for industrial or storage purposes — is unheated or has a space heating system with a design output rating not exceeding 50 W per square metre of floor area; or

        (ii)   in the case of any other building — is unheated or has a space heating system with a design output rating not exceeding 25 W per square metre of floor area.

(3)   In this Part—

SPACE HEATING SYSTEM and HOT WATER SUPPLY SYSTEM do not include a system or that part of a system which heats or stores water solely for a commercial or industrial process; and

PIPES AND DUCTS means any pipe and any duct in a space heating system or hot water supply system which is intended to carry a heated liquid or gas, and includes associated fittings.

F2   Conservation of fuel and power

Reasonable provision shall be made in the fabric of the building, or as the case may be, of the dwelling for the conservation of fuel and power.

F3 *Deemed-to-satisfy provision for conservation of fuel and power*

The requirements of regulation F2 shall be deemed to be satisfied if the design and construction of the building or dwelling are in accordance with DOE(NI) Technical Booklet F: 1991: Section 1.

F4 Control of space heating and hot water supply systems

Reasonable provision shall be made in any building or, as the case may be, in any dwelling for the purposes of the conservation of fuel and power to—

(a) regulate the output of a space heating system; and

(b) limit the temperature of stored hot water in a hot water supply system, by means of automatic controls.

F5 *Deemed-to-satisfy provision for control of space heating and hot water supply systems*

The requirements of regulation F4 shall be deemed to be satisfied if the space heating system and the hot water supply system is provided with controls which comply with DOE(NI) Technical Booklet F: 1991: Section 2.

F6 Insulation of pipes, ducts and hot water storage vessels

Reasonable provision shall be made to limit the heat loss from pipes, ducts and hot water storage vessels, other than that from a pipe or duct which is designed to contribute to the space heating of the space through which it passes.

F7 *Deemed-to-satisfy provision for the insulation of pipes, ducts and hot water storage vessels*

The requirements of regulation F6 shall be deemed to be satisfied if pipes, ducts and hot water storage vessels are insulated in accordance with DOE(NI) Technical Booklet F: 1991: Section 3.

Part G

Sound insulation of dwellings

G1 Application and interpretation

(1) This Part—

(a) applies only to a dwelling; but

(b) does not apply to a wall separating a dwelling from an open access balcony.

(2) Regulation G2 shall apply to the erection of a building and to the structural alteration or extension of an existing building.

(3) Regulation G4 shall apply to the material change of use of an existing building or part of an existing building.

(4) In this Part—

OPEN ACCESS BALCONY means a balcony which—

(a) gives access to dwellings or a common service area; and

(b) ignoring structural columns is open to the external air for more than one-third of its floor to ceiling height and throughout the length of the dwellings; and

SEPARATING WALL AND SEPARATING FLOOR mean respectively a wall or floor (including a stair) separating a dwelling from—

(a) another dwelling or another building; or

(b) another part of the same building which is not used exclusively with that dwelling.

G2 Separating walls and separating floors

(1) A separating wall in conjunction with its flanking construction shall provide adequate resistance to airborne sound transmission.

(2) Subject to paragraph (3) a separating floor in conjunction with its flanking construction shall provide adequate resistance to airborne sound transmission, and, where such a floor is above a dwelling, adequate resistance to impact sound transmission.

(3)   A separating floor or part of a separating floor which forms an open access balcony shall provide adequate resistance to impact sound transmission only.

G3   *Deemed-to-satisfy provisions for separating walls and separating floors*

The requirements of regulation G2 shall be deemed to be satisfied if the separating wall or separating floor in conjunction with its flanking construction is constructed in accordance with—

(a) *the Acceptable Construction Method contained in Section 1 of DOE(NI) Technical Booklet G: 1990; or*

(b) *the Similar Construction Method contained in Section 2 of DOE(NI) Technical Booklet G: 1990.*

G4   **Existing walls and floors which become separating walls and separating floors**

(1)   An existing wall which becomes a separating wall shall provide adequate resistance to airborne sound transmission.

(2)   Subject to paragraph (3) an existing floor or stair which becomes a separating floor shall provide adequate resistance to airborne sound transmission, and, where such a floor is above a dwelling, adequate resistance to impact sound transmission.

(3)   A separating floor or part of a separating floor which forms an open access balcony shall provide adequate resistance to impact sound transmission only.

G5   *Deemed-to-satisfy provisions for existing walls and floors which become separating walls and separating floors*

The requirements of regulation G4 shall be deemed to be satisfied if the separating wall or separating floor is constructed in accordance with—

(a) *the Essentially Similar Method contained in Section 1 of DOE(NI) Technical Booklet G1: 1994;*

(b) *the Acceptable Upgrading Method contained in Section 2 of DOE(NI) Technical Booklet G1: 1994; or*

(c) *one of the Similar Upgrading Methods contained in Section 3 of DOE(NI) Technical Booklet G1: 1994.*

Part H

Stairs, ramps and guarding

H1   Interpretation

In this Part—

BALCONY includes a gallery;

BARRIER includes a wall or screen;

FLIGHT means that part of a stair or ladder between landings that has a step or a continuous series of steps;

LADDER means a flight with a pitch greater than 55°;

LANDING means a platform situated—

(a) at the top or bottom of a stair or ramp; and

(b) between consecutive flights of a stair;

RAMP means an inclined surface which provides a route of travel; and

STAIR means a flight or flights (other than a ladder) and landings that make it possible to pass on foot to another level or levels.

H2   Provision of stairs in dwellings

Within every dwelling of more than one storey there shall be provided between such storeys access by means of a stair complying with the relevant provisions of this Part:

Provided that nothing in this regulation shall require the provision of a stair to any storey within a dwelling if that storey is used only as general storage accommodation.

H3   Stairs, ramps and landings

A stair, and a ramp and its landings, shall offer reasonable safety to people using them to move between—

(a) levels within the building (other than to or from a level used solely for the purpose of maintenance); and

(b) an entrance or exit of the building and the general ground level immediately outside that entrance or exit.

H4 *Deemed-to-satisfy provisions for stairs, ramps and landings*

The requirements of regulation H3 shall be deemed to be satisfied in the case of—

(a) *a stair – if it is constructed in accordance with DOE(NI) Technical Booklet H: 1994: Sections 1 and 2; and*

(b) *a ramp and its landings – if they are constructed in accordance with DOE(NI) Technical Booklet H: 1994: Sections 1 and 3.*

H5 Guarding

(1) Subject to paragraph (2) a stair, ramp, floor, balcony, landing, platform and any roof or other place to which people normally have access (other than for the purposes of maintenance) and a sunken area next to a building, shall, where it is necessary to protect people in or about the building from the risk of falling, be adequately guarded with a barrier which does not present a hazard.

(2) The requirements of paragraph (1) shall not apply—

(a) to the extent that compliance therewith would unreasonably obstruct normal movement into, out of or within any building;

(b) in relation to two steps at the bottom of a stair;

(c) in relation to a flight which is in a stair with a total rise of less than 600 mm; or

(d) in relation to a sunken area less than 600 mm in depth.

(3) Subject to paragraph (4) any part of a building which is a vehicle ramp, floor or roof to which vehicles have access shall, where it is necessary to protect people, be adequately guarded with a barrier which does not present a hazard.

(4) The requirements of paragraph (3) shall not apply in relation to a car showroom, a garage within the boundary of a dwelling, or a single storey building comprising two or more garages each of which has an area not exceeding 40 m².

H6 *Deemed-to-satisfy provisions for guarding*

(1) *The requirements of regulation H5(1) shall be deemed to be satisfied if the barrier complies with DOE(NI) Technical Booklet H: 1994: Section 4.*

(2) *The requirement of regulations H5(3) shall be deemed to be satisfied if the vehicle barrier is designed and constructed in accordance with the relevant recommendations of BS 6180: 1982.*

Part J

Solid waste in buildings

J1   Interpretation

In this Part—

INDIVIDUAL WASTE CONTAINER means a moveable container for the storage of waste from a single dwelling;

COMMUNAL WASTE CONTAINER means a moveable container for the storage of waste from more than one dwelling;

WASTE means solid waste; and

WASTE CHUTE SYSTEM means a system comprising of a hopper or hoppers, a waste chute, a waste container chamber and associated ventilation provisions.

J2   Solid waste storage

(1)   A building shall be provided with adequate space for the storage of waste in a container, and such space shall be—

(a) sited so as not to be prejudicial to the health of any person;

(b) sited so as to be reasonably accessible for use by people in the building in the storage of waste and for emptying or removing the container; and

(c) of sufficient capacity having regard to the quantity of waste and the frequency and method of removal.

(2)   Every dwelling—

(a) on or below the fourth storey of a building, shall have space for an individual waste container or access to a communal waste container or a waste chute system; and

(b) above the fourth storey of a building, shall have access to a waste chute system.

J3 *Deemed-to-satisfy provisions for the siting of waste containers and waste chute systems*

The requirements of regulation J2(1)(b) shall be satisfied if, in the case of—

(a) a dwelling not served by a waste chute system – the waste container space is—

    (i) a travel distance of not more than 30 m from the dwelling; and

    (ii) sited so that the waste container can be removed without being taken through that or any other building, other than a garage, carport or other open covered space; or

(b) a dwelling served by a waste chute system – the siting complies with the relevant clauses of BS 5906: 1980 (1987).

J4 **Waste chute systems**

A waste chute system shall—

(a) be of such size, layout and construction as will ensure the hygienic conveyance of waste to a waste container;

(b) be constructed of non-combustible materials;

(c) have non-absorbent inner surfaces;

(d) have adequate means of ventilation to the external air; and

(e) be so constructed as to prevent the ignition of any part of the building in the event of any waste within the system catching fire.

J5 *Deemed-to-satisfy provision for a waste chute system*

The requirements of regulation J4 shall be deemed to be satisfied if the waste chute system complies with the relevant clauses of BS 5906: 1980 (1987).

Part K

Ventilation

K1   Interpretation and application

(1)   In this Part—

BATHROOM means a room containing a bath or shower whether or not it also contains other sanitary appliances;

COMMON SPACE means a space intended for use by the occupants of more than one dwelling and not open to the external air;

HABITABLE ROOM has the meaning assigned to it by regulation A2 but does not include a room intended to be used for the lawful detention of any person other than a person of unsound mind; and

SANITARY APPLIANCE and SANITARY ACCOMMODATION have the meanings assigned to them by regulation P1.

(2)   Where sanitary accommodation contains a cubicle or cubicles constructed so as to allow free circulation of air throughout the room or space, then this Part shall apply to the room or space as a whole and not to the cubicle or cubicles separately.

K2   Means of ventilation

Adequate means of ventilation shall be provided for people using any habitable room, kitchen, bathroom, common space or sanitary accommodation in any building.

K3   *Deemed-to-satisfy provisions for ventilation*

(1)   In this regulation—

EXTRACT VENTILATION *means mechanical ventilation which extracts air from a room and discharges it only to the external air;*

MECHANICAL VENTILATION *means a system of ventilation operated by a power driven mechanism;* (air conditioning)

49

ROOM-SEALED APPLIANCE *means a heat-producing appliance which, when in operation, has its combustion air inlet and its combustion products outlet isolated from the room or space in which it is installed;*

TOP OF THE WALL *means—*

(a) *if the building has a flat roof, the underside of that roof;*

(b) *if the building has a pitched roof, the lowest part of the eaves of that roof; or*

(c) *if the roof (whether flat or pitched) has a parapet, the top of that parapet;*

TRICKLE VENTILATOR *means a small adjustable ventilation opening the sole purpose of which is to provide controllable background ventilation; and*

VENTILATION OPENING *means any part of a window, or any hinged panel, adjustable louvre or other means of ventilation which opens directly to the external air or, subject to paragraph (3), to an enclosed place, but does not include—*

(a) *any opening associated with a means of mechanical ventilation; or*

(b) *except in the circumstances described in paragraph (4), a door.*

(2) *The requirements of regulation K2 shall be deemed to be satisfied if the room or space specified in column (1) of the Table to this regulation has—*

(a) *either—*

    (i) *natural ventilation by means of—*

        (A) *one or more trickle ventilators having a total area of not less than that specified opposite thereto in column (2); and*

        (B) *one or more ventilation openings having a total area of not less than that specified opposite thereto in column (3); or*

    (ii) *mechanical ventilation capable of operating continuously at the rate specified opposite thereto in column (4); and*

(b) *extract ventilation capable of operating at a rate of not less than that specified opposite thereto in column (5):*

Provided that where a kitchen contains a heat-producing appliance, which is not a room-sealed appliance, and the heat-producing appliance burns —

    (i) *solid fuel; or*

    (ii) *gas or fuel oil, and it cannot be demonstrated that the operation of the extract ventilation will not cause spillage of combustion products or otherwise interfere with the safe operation of the heat-producing appliance,* extract ventilation shall not be provided and a ventilation opening having an area of not less than one-twentieth of the floor area of the kitchen shall be substituted therefor.

(3)   A ventilation opening provided for any room or space in accordance with paragraph (2) may open to an enclosed place only where that enclosed place—

(a) is a verandah, conservatory or similar place; and

(b) is ventilated directly to the external air by—

    (i)   one or more trickle ventilators having a total area of not less than that specified in column (2) of the Table to this regulation for that room or space; and

    (ii) one or more ventilation openings having a total area of not less than that specified in column (3) of the Table to this regulation for such a room or space having a floor area equal to the combined floor areas of the room or space and the enclosed place.

(4)   A door which opens directly to the external air shall only be regarded as a ventilation opening, for the purposes of this regulation, if—

(a) the door contains a ventilation opening with an area of not less than 10,000 mm^2 capable of being opened without the door being opened; or

(b) the room or space which it ventilates contains one or more ventilation openings having a total area of not less than 10,000 mm^2, in addition to the door and any ventilation openings in it.

(5)   No ventilation opening, other than a trickle ventilator constructed in compliance with the requirements of paragraph (2) shall be so situated as to open on to a court enclosed on every side, unless the distance from the ventilation opening to the opposite wall of the court is either—

(a) 15 m or more; or

(b) not less than half the vertical distance between the top of such opening and the top of the wall containing the opening.

(6)   No ventilation opening, other than a trickle ventilator constructed in compliance with the requirements of paragraph (2) shall be so situated as to open on to a court which has one side unobstructed by any building or other erection, and of which the long side, measured from such unobstructed side, exceeds twice the width, unless such ventilation opening—

(a) is in the side of the court opposite the unobstructed side;

(b) (if it is situated in either of the long sides) is within a distance from the unobstructed side not exceeding twice the width of the court; or

(c) (if it is situated in either of the long sides) is in such a position that the distance from the opening to the opposite wall of the court is either—

(i) 15 m or more; or

(ii) not less than half the vertical distance between the top of such opening and the top of the wall containing the opening.

Table to Regulation K3

Ventilation of rooms and spaces[+]

Room or Space (1)	Ventilation for RegulationK3(2)(a)			Ventilation for Regulation K3(2)(b)
	Natural ventilation		Mechanical ventilation	
	Minimum area of trickle ventilators (mm^2) (2)	Minimum area of ventilation openings# (3)	Number of air changes/ hour[†] (4)	Minimum rate of extract ventilation (litres/second) (5)
Habitable Room	4,000	1/20 of the floor area of the room	1	–
Kitchen‡	4,000	–	1	60^x
Sanitary Accommodation	–	1/20 of the floor area of the room	$3^\$$	–
Bathroom	–	–	–.	15^*
Common Space	–	1/50 of the floor area of the space	1	–

+ Additional ventilation may be required to a room containing a heat-producing appliance for the purposes of regulation L2.

Some part of such area shall be not less than 1.75 m above the floor.

† This is a nominal rate; the actual rate shall not vary by more than 25 per cent.

‡ These provisions apply to small kitchens such as those in dwellings.

x This rate is reduced to 30 litres/second when the extract ventilation is incorporated in a cooker hood.

$ The system may operate intermittently provided that it is capable of operating continuously while the room is in use and is fitted with a device which automatically continues its operation for a period of not less than 15 minutes after use ceases.

* The system shall be fitted with a device which automatically continues its operation for a period of not less than 15 minutes after it is switched off.

Notes to Table

(1)   Where a room is put to more than one use it shall be provided with ventilation which meets the requirements of the Table when each use is considered separately.

(2)   Mechanical ventilation under Column (4) and extract ventilation under Column (5) may be combined in a single system provided that the system is capable of continuous operation at the rate given in Column (4) and intermittent operation at the rate given in Column (5).

Part L

Heat – producing appliances and liquefied petroleum gas installations

L1 Interpretation and application

(1) In this Part—

CHIMNEY means a structure (not being a flue pipe, but including a factory made insulated chimney) enclosing one or more flues, but does not include any chimney pot or other flue terminal;

FLUE means a passage which conveys the combustion products from an appliance to the external air;

FLUE-PIPE means a pipe forming a flue, but not a pipe fitted as a lining in a chimney;

HEAT-PRODUCING APPLIANCE means a fixed appliance (including a cooker) which—

(a) is designed to burn solid fuel, gas, or oil; or

(b) is an incinerator;

LIQUEFIED PETROLEUM GAS (hereinafter referred to as LPG) means commercial butane and commercial propane in accordance with BS 4250: Part 1: 1987;

LPG INSTALLATION means an LPG storage tank and pipework, fittings, supports and all other items required to enable liquefied petroleum gas to be conveyed from the storage tank to the heat-producing appliance; and

LPG STORAGE TANK means a fixed bulk storage tank or vessel which is used for the storage of liquefied petroleum gas and is designed to be refilled in position.

(2) Any provision in regulation L2 which applies to a heat-producing appliance shall also apply where solid fuel is intended to burn directly on a hearth without the installation of any appliance.

(3) Regulation L5 applies to LPG installations which supply fuel to heat-producing appliances in a dwelling or other residential building, which is

not an institution, but not to an installation whose LPG storage tank is less than 150 litres or greater than 337,500 litres water capacity.

L2 Heat-producing appliances and associated constructions

(1) A heat-producing appliance shall be so installed that—

(a) it receives a sufficient supply of air to ensure the safe and efficient operation of the heat-producing appliance and any associated flue-pipe or chimney;

(b) combustion products discharged from the installation do not create a hazard to the health of any person;

(c) in the case of a heat-producing appliance designed to operate with a flue, combustion products are discharged to the external air through a flue-pipe or chimney complying with paragraph (2); and

(d) its use shall not cause damage to a building by heat or fire.

(2) Flue-pipes and chimneys shall be so constructed and installed that during operation of the heat-producing appliance to which they are connected they—

(a) ensure combustion products are discharged to the external air without creating a hazard to the health of any person; and

(b) prevent damage to a building by heat or fire.

(3) Hearths and fireplace recesses shall be so constructed and installed that they prevent damage to a building by heat or fire resulting from the operation of any heat-producing appliance installed therein or thereon.

L3 *Deemed-to-satisfy provisions for heat-producing appliances and associated constructions.*

The requirements of regulation L2 shall be deemed to be satisfied if the heat-producing appliances (other than incinerators) and associated constructions comply with, in the case of—

(a) solid fuel burning appliances having a rated output not exceeding 45 kW – DOE(NI) Technical Booklet L: 1991: Sections 1 and 2;

(b) gas-burning appliances having a rated input not exceeding 60 kW – DOE(NI) Technical Booklet L: 1991: Sections 1 and 3; and

(c) oil burning appliances having a rated output not exceeding 45 kW – DOE(NI) Technical Booklet L: 1991: Sections 1 and 4.

L4 Prevention of smoke emission

A heat-producing appliance installed in a building for the purpose of heating or cooking, and which discharges its combustion products to the external air shall be capable of, or readily adaptable to, the burning of fuel smokelessly, unless it is—

(a) a furnace which complies with Article 5 of the Clean Air (Northern Ireland) Order 1981**(a)** (which requires that new furnaces shall so far as practicable be smokeless); or

(b) an appliance of a class exempted conditionally or unconditionally from the provisions of Article 17 of that Order (which relates to smoke control areas) by any order for the time being in force under paragraph (7) of that Article.

L5 LPG fixed installations

The design, construction and installation of any LPG installation to which this regulation applies shall be safe and adequate for its purpose.

L6 *Deemed-to-satisfy provisions for LPG fixed installations*

The requirements of regulation L5 shall be deemed to be satisfied if—

(a) the LPG storage tank is sited in accordance with paragraphs 15 to 36;

(b) the mechanical integrity of the LPG storage tank is in accordance with paragraphs 37, 38 and 40;

(c) in the case of an underground or mounded LPG storage tank the installation is in accordance with paragraphs 41 to 46; and

(d) the pipework, fittings and supports are in accordance with paragraphs 58 to 89,

of Health and Safety Guidance Booklet HS(G) 34 published by the Health and Safety Executive: 1987.

L7 Separation distances from an existing LPG storage tank

A building shall be separated by a safe distance from any existing LPG storage tank within the same curtilage.

L8 *Deemed-to-satisfy provision for separation distances from an existing LPG storage tank*

The requirements of regulation L7 shall be deemed to be satisfied if the separation distances are in accordance with Table 2 of Health and Safety Guidance Booklet HS(G) 34 published by the Health and Safety Executive: 1987, and, where a fire wall is provided, paragraphs 34 to 36 of the Booklet.

(a) S.I. 1981 No 158 (NI 4)

Part N

Drainage

N1 Interpretation and application

(1) In this Part—

FOUL WATER means waste from a sanitary appliance and water which has been used for cooking or washing purposes and not contaminated by trade effluent;

RAIN-WATER DRAINAGE includes gutters, pipes, drains and fittings which convey rain-water only;

SANITARY APPLIANCE has the meaning assigned to it by regulation P1;

SANITARY PIPEWORK means a pipe or system of pipes for conveying foul water from a fitting to an underground foul drain; and

UNDERGROUND FOUL DRAINAGE includes drains and private sewers used in connection with buildings but not a system which is solely for the conveyance of subsurface water.

(2) Regulation N7 shall not apply to a drainage system intended for use in connection with a roof or balcony of 6 m^2 or less in area, unless that roof or balcony receives a flow of rain-water from another part of a building.

N2 Drainage systems

Every building shall be provided with such sanitary pipework, underground foul drainage and rain-water drainage as may be necessary for the hygienic and adequate disposal of foul water and rain-water from that building.

N3 Sanitary pipework

Sanitary pipework shall—

(a) consist of pipes and fittings—

    (i)   of such size, layout, construction and watertightness; and

(ii)   with sufficient ventilation,

to ensure the hygienic conveyance of foul water to an underground foul drainage system; and

(b) have such means of access as is necessary to facilitate the clearance of blockages.

N4   Deemed-to-satisfy provision for sanitary pipework

The requirements of regulation N3 shall be deemed to be satisfied if the sanitary pipework complies with DOE(NI) Technical Booklet N: 1990: Section 1.

N5   Underground foul drainage

Underground foul drainage shall—

(a) consist of pipes and fittings—

(i)   of such size, layout, construction and watertightness; and

(ii)   with sufficient ventilation,

to ensure the hygienic conveyance of foul water to a sewer, cesspool, septic tank or similar structure; and

(b) have such means of access as is necessary to facilitate the clearance of blockages.

N6   Deemed-to-satisfy provision for underground foul drainage

The requirements of regulation N5 shall be deemed to be satisfied if the underground foul drainage complies with DOE(NI) Technical Booklet N: 1990: Section 2.

N7   Rain-water drainage

Rain-water drainage shall—

(a) consist of pipes and fittings—

(i)   of such size, layout, construction and watertightness; and

(ii)   with sufficient ventilation,

to ensure the hygienic conveyance of rain-water to a surface water or combined sewer, a soakaway or a watercourse; and

(b) have such means of access as is necessary to facilitate the clearance of blockages.

N8   Deemed-to-satisfy provision for rain-water drainage

The requirements of regulation N7 shall be deemed to be satisfied if the rain-water drainage complies with DOE(NI) Technical Booklet N: 1990: Section 3.

N9 Cesspools, septic tanks and similar structures

(1) Any cesspool, septic tank or similar structure shall be—

(a) so constructed as to be impervious to both liquid from the inside and subsoil water from the outside; and

(b) so sited—

(i) as not to render liable to pollution any spring, stream, well, adit, or other source of water which is used, or is likely to be used, for drinking, domestic or kitchen purposes;

(ii) that there is ready means of access for cleansing it and removing its contents without carrying them through any building in which any person resides or is employed in any manufacture, trade or business, or to which the public has access; and

(iii) as not to be in such proximity to any building in which any person resides or is employed in any manufacture, trade or business, or to which the public has access, as to be liable to become a source of nuisance or a danger to health.

(2) A cesspool shall be—

(a) of suitable depth to enable it to be emptied completely;

(b) properly covered so as to be impervious to surface water and rain-water;

(c) fitted with a suitable manhole cover for the purposes of inspection (including inspection of the inlet), emptying and cleansing;

(d) adequately ventilated;

(e) without any outlet for overflow or discharge other than the outlet provided for emptying or cleansing; and

(f) of a capacity, measured below the level of the inlet, of not less than 18 m³.

(3) Any structure to which paragraph (1) applies other than a cesspool shall be—

(a) of suitable depth;

(b) of adequate size, having in no case a capacity of less than 2.7 m³;

(c) covered or fenced in;

(d) if covered, adequately ventilated and constructed with means of access for the purposes of inspection (including inspection of the inlet and outlet), emptying and cleansing; and

(e) fitted with filter or other treatment facility for effluent (including subsurface irrigation) or both, sited to comply with the requirements of paragraph (1)(b)(i) and (iii).

Part P

Sanitary appliances and unvented hot water storage systems

P1   Interpretation

In this Part—

DOMESTIC HOT WATER means water that has been heated for ablution, culinary and cleansing purposes irrespective of the type of building;

SANITARY ACCOMMODATION means a room or space which contains a water closet or urinal whether or not it also contains other sanitary appliances;

SANITARY APPLIANCES includes a water closet or urinal and a bath, shower, wash-hand basin, bidet or other fitting for ablutionary purposes;

SANITARY PIPEWORK AND UNDERGROUND FOUL DRAINAGE have the meanings assigned to them by regulation N1; and

URINAL includes one or more slabs, stalls, troughs, bowls or other suitable receptacles.

P2   Provision of sanitary appliances

(1)   A dwelling shall have at least one water closet, one wash-hand basin and one fixed bath or shower.

(2)   A wash-hand basin shall be provided, in the case of—

(a) a dwelling – either in the same room as a water closet or in an adjacent room; and

(b) any other building – either in the same room as a water closet or in an adjoining room which provides the sole means of access to the room containing the water closet.

(3)   A water closet fitted with a macerator shall not be provided in any building unless the building has another water closet, accessible to all occupants, which discharges directly to sanitary pipework or underground foul drainage.

P3 Sanitary appliances

(1) Every sanitary appliance shall have smooth and readily cleansed, non-absorbent surfaces and shall discharge through an effective trap of suitable dimensions.

(2) Every wash-hand basin, bath and shower shall have provision for the piped supply of hot and cold water and where a sequential single control mixer valve is provided it shall start from the cold supply.

(3) Every water closet and urinal shall have flushing apparatus capable of effectively cleansing the receptacle, no part of which shall be directly connected to any pipe other than a flush pipe or sanitary pipework.

(4) The outlet of a urinal shall have an effective grating.

(5) A sanitary appliance fitted with a macerator, pump and drainage pipe shall ensure the hygienic conveyance of foul water to an underground foul drainage system.

P4 Sanitary accommodation

(1) Sanitary accommodation shall not open directly into—
   (a) a habitable room unless the room is used solely for sleeping or dressing purposes;
   (b) a room used for kitchen purposes; or
   (c) a room in which a person is habitually employed in any trade or business.

(2) Any sanitary accommodation which can be entered directly from a room used for sleeping purposes, shall be so constructed that it can also be entered without passing through any such room, but this paragraph shall not apply if in the case of—
   (a) a dwelling – there is other such sanitary accommodation within the dwelling which can be entered without passing through any such room; or
   (b) any other building – there is within the building other such sanitary accommodation which is available for common use.

P5 Unvented hot water storage systems

(1) This regulation shall apply to any hot water storage system (other than a system or part of a system used solely for space heating or an industrial process) that has a storage vessel which—
   (a) has a capacity greater than 15 litres; and
   (b) does not incorporate a vent pipe to the atmosphere.

(2) A hot water storage system to which this regulation applies, whether heated directly or indirectly, shall incorporate—

(a) safety devices to ensure that the temperature of the stored water does not exceed 100°C at any time; and

(b) devices to control the working pressure and to relieve excessive pressure.

(3) Any discharge from devices provided for the purpose of paragraph (2) shall be conveyed safely to where it can be seen readily and will cause no danger to persons.

P6 *Deemed-to-satisfy provision for an unvented domestic hot water storage system*

The requirements of regulation P5 shall be deemed to be satisfied in relation to a domestic hot water storage system to which that regulation applies if the system is designed, constructed and installed in accordance with DOE(NI) Technical Booklet P: 1994.

Part R

Access and facilities for disabled people

R1 Application and interpretation

(1) Subject to paragraph (2) this Part shall apply to any building or part of a building.

(2) This Part shall not apply to—

(a) a dwelling (including any associated garage or outbuilding), other than any part of the ground storey of the dwelling which is used as, or in connection with, a surgery for the treatment of patients;

(b) the common parts of a building which are intended for the exclusive use of two or more dwellings; and

(c) any part of a building which is used solely to enable the building or any service or fitting in the building to be inspected, maintained or repaired.

(3) In this Part—

DISABLED PEOPLE means people who have—

(a) an impairment which limits their ability to walk or which requires them to use a wheelchair for mobility; or

(b) impaired hearing or sight; and

SANITARY ACCOMMODATION has the meaning assigned to it in regulation P1.

R2 Access and use

Reasonable provision shall be made for disabled people to have access to and within and to use any building or part of a building to which this Part applies.

R3 *Deemed-to-satisfy provisions for access and use*

The requirements of regulation R2 shall be deemed to be satisfied if the provisions for access and use comply with, in the case of—

(a) *an educational building – the relevant provisions of the Department of Education and Science Design Note 18 (1984), Access for Disabled People to Educational Buildings; or*

(b) *any other building – DOE(NI) Technical Booklet R: 1994: Sections 1, 2, 3 and 4.*

R4 Sanitary accommodation

If sanitary accommodation is provided in a building, other than in a shop which has a floor area of less than 50 m², reasonable sanitary accommodation shall also be provided for disabled people.

R5 *Deemed-to-satisfy provisions for sanitary accommodation*

The requirements of regulation R4 shall be deemed to be satisfied if the sanitary accommodation complies with, in the case of such accommodation in—

(a) *an educational building – the relevant provisions of the Department of Education and Science Design Note 18 (1984), Access for Disabled People to Educational Buildings; or*

(b) *any other building – DOE(NI) Technical Booklet R: 1994: Sections 1 and 5.*

R6 Audience or spectator seating

If a building contains audience or spectator seating, reasonable provision shall be made to accommodate disabled people.

R7 *Deemed-to-satisfy provision for audience or spectator seating*

The requirements of regulation R6 shall be deemed to be satisfied if audience or spectator seating complies with DOE(NI) Technical Booklet R: 1994: Sections 1 and 6.

Part V

Glazing

V1 Glazing

Glazing in a building with which people are likely to come into contact while in passage in or about the building shall—

(a) if broken on impact, break in a way which is unlikely to cause injury;

(b) resist reasonable impact without breaking; or

(c) be shielded or protected from impact.

V2 *Deemed-to-satisfy provision for glazing*

The requirements of regulation V1 shall be deemed to be satisfied if the glazing complies with DOE(NI) Technical Booklet V: 1994: Sections 1 and 2.

V3 Transparent glazing

In a building or part of a building, other than in a dwelling, transparent glazing, of which people may otherwise be unaware and with which they are likely to collide while in passage in or about the building, shall incorporate features which make it apparent.

V4 *Deemed-to-satisfy provision for transparent glazing*

The requirements of regulation V3 shall be deemed to be satisfied if the transparent glazing complies with DOE(NI) Technical Booklet V: 1994: Section 3.

Sealed with the Official Seal of the Department of the Environment on 28th June 1994.

(L.S.)

J. O'Neill
Assistant Secretary

SCHEDULES

SCHEDULE 1

Part A – Partially exempted buildings
Regulation A5(2)

1. The provisions of these regulations, other than those provisions listed in paragraph 2, shall not apply to—

    (a) a conservatory with a floor area not exceeding 30 m^2 which is attached to a dwelling;

    (b) an attached greenhouse with a floor area not exceeding 30 m^2; or

    (c) a porch with a floor area not exceeding 8 m^2 which is built as an annexe to an existing building:

    Provided in all cases that—

    (i) the structure is not less than 1 m from a boundary; and

    (ii) its floor is at or about the level of the ground adjoining the building or the level of the ground storey of the building to which it is attached.

2. The relevant requirements of the following provisions of these regulations shall apply to buildings partially exempted by paragraph 1—

    In Part A (Interpretation and general) regulations A10 and A11

    Part B (Materials and workmanship) insofar as it relates to work to which any regulation in this paragraph applies

    In Part C (Preparation of site and resistance to moisture) regulations C1 and C2(2)

    In Part E (Fire safety) regulations E4 and E8(b)

    In Part H (Stairs, ramps and guarding) regulations H3 and H5

    In Part K (Ventilation) regulation K2

    In Part L (Heat-producing appliances and LPG installations) regulations L2 and L7

    In Part N (Drainage) regulation N7

    Part V (Glazing) in respect of conservatories and porches only.

SCHEDULE 1 – continued

Part B – Classes of wholly exempted buildings
Regulation A5(1)

In Classes 2 and 3 of this Part HEIGHT shall be measured from the lowest level of the ground adjoining the building to the highest point of the building.

Class	Description of wholly exempted building
(1)	(2)

1   **Buildings controlled under other legislation**

    (a) Any building the construction of which is subject to the Explosives Acts (Northern Ireland) 1875 and 1924**(a)**.

    (b) Any building (other than a building containing a dwelling or a building used for office or canteen accommodation) erected on a site in respect of which a licence under the Nuclear Installations Act 1965**(b)** is for the time being in force.

    (c) A building being any monument for the time being subject to Parts I, II or III of the Historic Monuments Act (Northern Ireland) 1971**(c)** other than any such building or part thereof which is used as residential accommodation or as an institution.

2   **Buildings not frequented by people**

A detached building into which people do not normally go, or into which people go only intermittently and then only for the purpose of inspecting or maintaining fixed plant or machinery, unless any point of such a building is less than one and a half times its height from—

    (i) any point of a building into which people can or do normally go;

    (ii) the nearest part of a road; or

    (iii) the nearest point of the boundary of the land on which the building is to be erected.

3   **Buildings for agriculture and keeping of animals**

A building used for agriculture, but not including a building used principally for retailing (including storage for retailing), packaging, exhibiting or as an office, provided that—

    (i) no part of the building is used as a dwelling;

(a) 1875 c17, 1924 c.5 (NI)
(b) 1965 c57; the only relevant amending instrument is SI 1974/2056
(c) 1971 c17 (NI)

Class	Description of wholly exempted building
(1)	(2)

3   **Buildings for agriculture and keeping of animals (continued)**

(ii) no point of the building is less than one and half times its height from—

    (A) any point of a building which contains sleeping accommodation;

    (B) the nearest part of a road; or

    (C) the nearest point of the boundary of the land on which it is to be erected; and

(iii) the building is provided with a fire exit which is not more than 30 m from any point in the building.

4   **Temporary buildings**

A building, including an exhibition stand and a stand for viewing a public display, which is not intended to remain where it is erected for more than 28 days.

5   **Ancillary buildings**

(a) A building on a construction site, being a building which is intended to be used only in connection with the disposal of buildings or building plots on that site and which contains no sleeping accommodation.

(b) A building on or close to the site of construction or civil engineering work, which is intended to be used only by people engaged on those works during the course of those works and which contains no sleeping accommodation.

(c) A building, other than a building containing a dwelling or used as an office or showroom, erected for use on the site of and in connection with a mine or quarry.

6   **Small detached buildings**

(a) A detached single storey building, having a floor area which does not exceed 30 m^2, which contains no sleeping accommodation and is a building which is either—

    (i) constructed substantially of non-combustible material; or

    (ii) at no point less than 1 m from–

        (A) the nearest point of a dwelling;

        (B) the nearest part of a road; or

        (C) the nearest point of the boundary of the land on which it is to be erected.

(b) A detached building designed and intended to shelter people from the effects of nuclear, chemical or conventional weapons, and not used for any other purpose, if—

    (i) its floor area does not exceed 30 m^2; and

    (ii) the excavation for the building is no closer to any exposed part of another building or structure than a distance equal to the depth of the excavation plus 1 m.

(c) A detached single storey building, having a floor area which does not exceed 15 m^2, which contains no sleeping accommodation and is not less than 1 m from a dwelling.

Schedule 1

Class	Description of wholly exempted building
(1)	(2)

7 **Extensions**

The extension of a dwelling by the addition at ground level of a covered way or covered area (including a carport) provided that the extension is open on at least two sides and its floor area does not exceed 30 m².

8 **Other buildings**

(a) An air-supported structure which—

    (i) does not exceed 15 m in length or diameter;

    (ii) has alternative means of escape;

    (iii) is not less than 2 m from any building to which these regulations apply; and

    (iv) is used solely in connection with a dwelling.

(b) An air-supported structure which—

    (i) after deflation is re-erected in accordance with plans previously approved and with any conditions imposed in connection with the approval of those plans; and

    (ii) is used for the same purpose as that for which it was previously erected.

(c) A tent or marquee.

(d) A movable dwelling including a tent, caravan, shed or similar structure used for human habitation.

(e) Mobile accommodation used in a static condition, including a houseboat, caravan or railway carriage.

(f) Any part of a dock, wharf, pier, lighthouse, dam, reservoir, railway line, airfield, pavement, canal (including locks and other structures associated therewith), oil rig, tunnel, bridge, road, path, ramp, stairway, walkway or work of public utility which does not form part of, give support to or gain support from, a building to which these regulations apply and which is not required for the purposes of Part R of these regulations; sewage disposal works other than buildings designed to house plant or provide covered accommodation for persons.

(g) A structure (other than a chimney) not incorporating any covered space with headroom exceeding 1.5 m, except where the structure is attached to or within a building to which these regulations apply; a tower mast not attached to a building to which these regulations apply.

(h) Unclad plant or machinery, including a vending or weighing machine.

(i) Amusement, playground or fairground equipment, including a swing, roundabout and scenic railway.

(j) Scaffolding, falsework, lifts and hoists used in association with engineering or construction work.

(k) Storage racking not incorporating a floor.

(l) Road barriers, street furniture or similar structures, including a traffic light or sign.

(m) A fence, wall or gate not forming part of a building to which these regulations apply.

(n) An external storage tank, not being a septic tank, settlement tank, cesspool, liquefied petroleum gas storage tank or tower silo.

(o) Gantries or galleries used solely for access to or the operation of plant or machinery.

SCHEDULE 2

Giving of notices and deposit of plans
Regulation A10

Rule A: General

The following provisions shall be observed in relation to the giving of any notices and the deposit of any plans, sections, specifications and particulars referred to in the other rules of this Schedule:

1. Notices and other particulars shall be in writing.

2. Drawings shall be executed or reproduced in a clear and intelligible manner with suitable and durable materials. Plans and sections shall be to a scale of not less than 1:100 or, if the building is so extensive as to render a smaller scale necessary, not less than 1:200; block plans shall be to a scale of not less than 1:1250; and key plans shall be to a scale of not less than 1:2500. The scale shall be indicated on all plans, sections and other drawings and the north point on all block plans and key plans.

3. Every notice, drawing or other document shall be signed by the person required to furnish it to the district council or by his duly authorised agent, and in all cases shall state the full name and address of the person on whose behalf it has been furnished.

4. Every such document, together with a duplicate thereof, shall be sent or delivered to the offices of the district council and the district council may retain one copy.

5. Where the building, or part thereof, is put or is intended to be put to a use which is a designated use for the purposes of the Fire Services (Northern Ireland) Order 1984(a) a statement to that effect, accompanied by a further 2 copies of such plans as demonstrate compliance with the requirements of Part E (Fire safety) of these regulations, shall be deposited with the district council which may retain both such copies.

Rule B: Erection of buildings (other than wholly or partially exempted buildings)

The following are the notices to be given and the plans, specifications and particulars to be deposited by a person intending to erect a building which is neither wholly nor partially exempted from the operation of these regulations under regulation A5:

1. Notice of intention to erect a building not wholly or partially exempted from the operation of these regulations.

2. Particulars, so far as necessary to show whether the building complies with all such requirements of these regulations as apply to it, of—

    (a) the intended use of the building;

    (b) the materials of which the building will be constructed;

    (c) the mode of drainage; and

    (d) the means of water supply.

(a) SI 1984 No 1821 (NI 11)

Schedule 2

3. A block plan showing—

    (a) the size and position of the building and its relationship to adjoining buildings;

    (b) the width and position of every street adjoining the premises; and

    (c) the boundaries of the premises and the size and position of every other building and of every road, path, garden, yard and other open space within such boundaries.

4. A key plan showing the position of the site when it is not sufficiently identifiable from the block plan.

5. A plan of every floor and roof of the building and a section of every storey of the building, upon which shall be shown (where not already shown on the particulars and plans required by items 2 to 4), so far as necessary to enable the district council to determine whether the building complies with these regulations—

    (a) the levels of the site of the building, of the lowest floor of the building and of any street adjoining the premises, in relation to one another and above some known datum;

    (b) the position of the damp-proof courses and any other barriers to moisture;

    (c) the position, form and dimensions of the foundations, walls, windows, floors, roofs, chimneys and several parts of the building;

    (d) the intended use of every room in the building;

    (e) the provision made in the structure for protection against fire;

    (f) the provision made in the building or part of the building for means of escape in case of fire and for securing that such means can be safely and effectively used at all material times; and

    (g) the provision made in the structure for insulation against the transmission of heat and sound.

Rule C: Erection of partially exempted buildings

The following are the notices to be given and the plans, specifications and particulars to be deposited by a person intending to erect a building partially exempted from the operation of these regulations under regulation A5:

1. Notice of intention to erect a building partially exempted from the operation of these regulations.

2. Particulars, so far as necessary, to show that the building falls within Part A Schedule 1 and whether the building complies with all such requirements of these regulations as apply to it, of –

    (a) the intended use of the building;

    (b) the materials of which the building will be constructed; and

    (c) the mode of drainage.

3. A block plan showing the size and position of the building and its relationship to adjoining buildings and indicating its distance from the boundary of the premises.

4. A key plan showing the position of the site when it is not sufficiently identifiable from the block plan.

5. Plans and sections of the partially exempted building and the existing building, showing the particulars required by item 5(a) to (f) of Rule B so far as may be necessary to enable the district council to determine whether the building complies with these regulations.

Rule D: Alterations and extensions

The following are the notices to be given and the plans, sections, specifications and particulars to be deposited by a person intending to make any alteration of or extension to a building other than an alteration or extension which is wholly exempted from these regulations:

1. Notice of intention to alter or extend a building.

2. In the case of alterations not involving any extension of a building—

    (a) the plans and sections required by item 5 of either Rule B or Rule C (whichever is appropriate) of the alterations and of the building so far as affected by the alterations, so far as necessary to establish whether the proposals comply with these regulations; and

    (b) a key plan showing the position of the site when it is not sufficiently identifiable from such plans.

3. In the case of an extension of a building—

    (a) the plans, sections, specifications and particulars referred to in items 2, 3, 4 and 5 of either Rule B or Rule C (whichever is appropriate) in relation to the extension as if the extension was the building therein referred to; and

    (b) the plans and sections as required by item 5 of either Rule B or Rule C (whichever is appropriate) of the building so far as affected by the extension,

    so far as necessary to enable the district council to determine whether the proposals comply with the requirements of these regulations.

Rule E: Services and fittings

The following are the notices to be given and the plans, sections, specifications and written particulars to be deposited by a person intending to provide any services or fittings to which regulation A8 relates:

1. Notice of intention to provide any services or fittings in connection with a building.

2. (a) Particulars of the services or fittings so far as is necessary to establish whether they comply with all such requirements of these regulations as apply to them; and

    (b) where it is proposed to provide an unvented hot water storage system to which Part P of these regulations apply, the particulars required by paragraph (a) shall include—

    (i) the name, make, model and type of hot water storage system to be installed;

    (ii) the name of the body, if any, which has approved or certified that the system is capable of performing in a way which satisfies the requirements of Part P; and

    (iii) the name of the body, if any, which has issued any current registered operative identity card to the installer or proposed installer of the system.

3. Where it is proposed to execute works of drainage or to construct or install a water closet fitting, urinal fitting, cesspool, septic tank or similar structure (for the reception or disposal of foul water from buildings), a block plan. Such plan shall, if the work is in connection with an operation to which Rule B, C or D relates, be the block plan required by such rule and the block plan shall in any case show, so far as necessary to establish whether the proposals comply with all such requirements of these regulations as apply to them—

    (a) the position of services or fittings;

    (b) the lines of drainage; the size, depth and inclination of every drain and the means of access to be provided for the inspection and clearance of blockages;

(c) the position and level of the outfall of the drains; and

(d) where the drainage is intended to be connected to a sewer, the position of the sewer.

4. Where it is proposed to construct or install a water closet fitting, urinal fitting, cesspool, septic tank or similar structure (for the reception or disposal of foul water from buildings), plans and sections of the works or fittings, so far as necessary to show that they comply with all such requirements of these regulations as apply to them.

5. A key plan showing the position of the site when it is not sufficiently identifiable from the block plan.

Rule F: Material changes of use

The following are the notices to be given and the plans, specifications and particulars to be deposited by a person intending to make any material change of use to which these regulations are applied by regulation A9, in addition to anything required by Rule D in a case to which that rule relates:

1. Notice of intention to make, and description of, any change in the purposes for which the building or part of the building is used.

2. A block plan showing the size and position of the building and its relationship to adjoining buildings.

3. A key plan showing the position of the site when it is not sufficiently identifiable from the block plan.

4. The provision made in the structure for protection against fire; and the provisions made in the building or part of a building for means of escape in case of fire and for securing that such means can be safely and effectively used at all material times.

5. In the case of a material change of use involving an increase in imposed loadings, the plans and sections required by item 5(c) and (d) of Rule B.

Rule G: Additional requirements

Where it is considered necessary for the purpose of examining any proposals submitted in accordance with Rule B, C, D or F, an authorised officer of the district council may require the deposit of any of the following drawings and particulars in addition to plans, sections, specifications and particulars required by such rule:

1. A specification of any particular material or materials proposed to be used.

2. The proportions of the materials in any concrete or mortar or the specified minimum strength of the concrete or mortar.

3. Calculations of loading and strength:

   Provided that where the dimensions of a structural member accord with the provisions of DOE(NI) Technical Booklet D: 1994 calculations of strength to demonstrate the adequacy of those dimensions shall not be required.

4. Drawings showing details of particular construction.

5. Calculations relating to the space separation of buildings for the purposes of regulation E8.

6. Calculations for the purposes of regulation E2.

7. Calculations for the purposes of regulation F2.

8. Soil investigation report.

9. Details of measures proposed for protection against radon.

SCHEDULE 3

Publications to which specific reference is made in the Building Regulations (Northern Ireland) 1994.
Regulation A2(10)(b)

Table A. British Standards

Publication	Amendment Slip		Context
	Serial Number	Reference Number	
(1)	(2)	(3)	(4)
BS 449: Part 2: 1969	1	AMD 416	D3(c)
	2	AMD 523	
	3	AMD 661	
	4	AMD 1135	
	5	AMD 1787	
	6	AMD 4576	
	7	AMD 5698	
	8	AMD 6255	
BS 4250: Part 1: 1987	—	—	L1(1)
BS 5250: 1989	—	—	C8
BS 5268: Part 2: 1991	—	—	D3(g)
BS 5268: Part 3: 1985	1	AMD 5931	D3(g)
BS 5588: Part 1: 1990	1	AMD 7840	E3(b)
BS 5588: Part 2: 1985	1	AMD 5555	E3(h)(ii)
	2	AMD 6239	
	3	AMD 6478	
BS 5588: Part 3: 1983	1	AMD 5556	E3(g)(ii)
	2	AMD 5825	
	3	AMD 6160	
BS 5588: Part 6: 1991	—	—	E3(j)(ii)
BS 5588: Part 8: 1988	—	—	E3(g),(h),(i),(j),(k) and (m)
BS 5588: Part 10: 1991	—	—	E3(i) E7(a)
BS 5589: 1989	—	—	B4(2)
BS 5617: 1985	—	—	B5(2)
BS 5618: 1985	1	AMD 6262	B5(2)
	2	AMD 7114	
BS 5628: Part 1: 1992	1	AMD 7745	D3(f) D5
BS 5628: Part 2: 1985	—	—	D3(f)
BS 5628: Part 3: 1985	1	AMD 4974	D3(f)

Schedule 3

Table A. British Standards – continued

Publication	Amendment Slip		Context
	Serial Number	Reference Number	
(1)	(2)	(3)	(4)
BS 5906: 1980 (1987)	—	—	J3(b) J5
BS 5950: Part 1: 1990	1	AMD 6972	D3(c) D5(2)(a)(ii)
BS 5950: Part 2: 1992	1	AMD 7766	D3(c)
BS 5950: Part 3: Section 3.1 1990	—	—	D3(d)
BS 5950: Part 4: 1982 and 1994	—	—	D3(c)
BS 5950: Part 5: 1987	1	AMD 5957	D3(c)
BS 6180: 1982	1	AMD 4858	H6(2)
BS 6399: Part 1: 1984	1 2 3	AMD 4949 AMD 5881 AMD 6031	D1(a)
BS 6399: Part 3: 1988	1	AMD 6033	D1(b)
BS 8004: 1986	—	—	D3(a)
BS 8110: Part 1: 1985	1 2 3 4	AMD 5917 AMD 6276 AMD 7583 AMD 7973	D3(b) D5
BS 8110: Part 2: 1985	1	AMD 5914	D3(b) D5
BS 8110: Part 3: 1985	1	AMD 5918	D3(b)
BS 8118: Part 1: 1991	—	—	D3(e)
BS 8118: Part 2: 1991	—	—	D3(e)

SCHEDULE 3 — continued

Table B. British Standard Codes of Practice

Publication (1)	Amendment Slip		Context (4)
	Serial Number (2)	Reference Number (3)	
CP3: Chapter V: Part 2: 1972	1 2 3 4 5	AMD 4952 AMD 5152 AMD 5343 AMD 6028 AMD 7908	D1(c)
CP 118: 1969	1	AMD 1129	D3(e)

SCHEDULE 3 — continued

Table C. Other Publications

Publication	Amendment	Context
(1)	(2)	(3)
DOE(NI) Technical Booklet C: 1994	—	C6
DOE(NI) Technical Booklet D: 1994	—	D5, D3 Schedule 2, Rule G (3)
DOE(NI) Technical Booklet E: 1994	—	E3(a),(g),(h),(j) and (m) E5 E7(b) E9 E11
DOE(NI) Technical Booklet F: 1991	—	F3 F5 F7
DOE(NI) Technical Booklet G: 1990	—	G3
DOE(NI) Technical Booklet G1: 1994	—	G5
DOE(NI) Technical Booklet H: 1994	—	H4(a),(b) H6(1)
DOE(NI) Technical Booklet L: 1991	—	L3
DOE(NI) Technical Booklet N: 1990	—	N4 N6 N8
DOE(NI) Technical Booklet P: 1994	—	P6
DOE(NI) Technical Booklet R: 1994	—	R3(b) R5(b) R7
DOE(NI) Technical Booklet V: 1994	—	V2 V4
EC Directive 89/106/EEC	—	A2(1)
Educational Buildings:– Building Bulletin 7 published by Department of Education and Science: 1988	—	E3(k)
Educational Buildings:– Department of Education and Science Design Note 18 (1984) "Access for Disabled People to Educational Buildings"	—	R3(a) R5(a)

Table C. Other Publications – continued

Publication	Amendment	Context
(1)	(2)	(3)
Hospitals:– Draft Guide to Fire Precautions in Hospitals published by the Home Office: 1982	—	E3(c)(iii)
Hospitals:– Health Technical Memorandum 81 published by the Department of Health and Social Security: 1989	—	E3(c)(i)
Hospitals:– Nucleus Fire Precautions Recommendations published by the Department of Health: 1989	—	E3(c)(ii)
Hotels:– Guide to Fire Precautions in Premises used as Hotels and Boarding Houses which require a Fire Certificate, published by the Home Office 1991	—	E3(f)
Houses in multiple occupation:– DOE Circular 12/92 published by the Department of the Environment: 1992	—	E3(e)
LPG:– Health and Safety Guidance Booklet HS (G)34 published by the Health and Safety Executive: 1987	—	L6 L8
Residential Care:– Draft Guide to Fire Precautions in Existing Residential Care Premises published by the Home Office: 1983	—	E3(d)(ii)
Residential Care:– Health Technical Memorandum 88 published by the Department of Health and Social Security: 1986	—	E3(d)(i)
Sports Grounds:– Guide to Safety at Sports Grounds published by Home Office: 1990	—	E3(l)

SCHEDULE 4

Map of radon affected zones
Regulation C2(2)

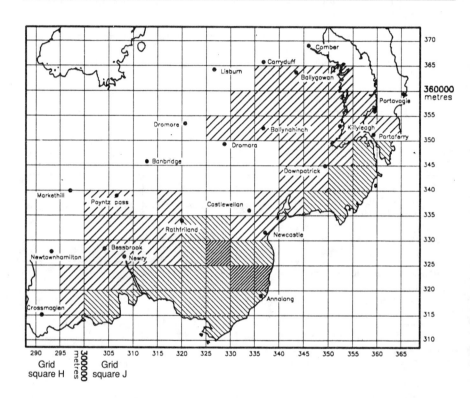

KEY TO MAP

 Zone A – 1% to 3% probability of radon concentration exceeding 200 becquerels per cubic metre.

 Zone B – 3% to 10% probability of radon concentration exceeding 200 becquerels per cubic metre.

 Zone C – Greater than 10% probability of radon concentration exceeding 200 becquerels per cubic metre.

NOTES TO MAP

The grid shown on the map is the Irish Grid established by Ordnance Survey of Northern Ireland.

EXPLANATORY NOTE

(This note is not part of the Regulations)

These Regulations revoke and replace with amendments the Building Regulations (Northern Ireland) 1990 ("the 1990 Regulations"), and all subsequent amending Regulations. They apply, in whole or in part, and subject to exceptions, to –

(a) the construction of any building and to certain services and fittings in conjunction with any building;

(b) the structural alteration or extension of any building; and

(c) any building undergoing a material change of use.

They come into operation on 28 November 1994, but do not apply in relation to work which has been completed, or for which plans have been deposited with a district council, before that date.

As in the previous Building Regulations, each Part of these Regulations is identified by a capital letter and the Regulations within each Part are identified by the appropriate letter and by numbers which run from "1" within each Part.

Some of the mandatory requirements of the Regulations are complemented by provisions which describe methods or materials which are deemed to satisfy the relevant functional or performance requirements. These provisions (called "deemed-to-satisfy provisions" and printed in italics) make extensive use of British Standards, British Standard Codes of Practice and, where relevant DOE (NI) Technical Booklets. In addition–

(a) any products designed and manufactured in accordance with a European Council Directive relating to a particular purpose shall be deemed to satisfy the requirements of these Regulations insofar as they relate to that purpose; and

(b) any products designed and manufactured in accordance with–

(i) any national technical specification of a state within the European Economic Area;

(ii) any relevant international standard recognised for use within such a state;

(iii) any appropriate traditional procedures of manufacture used within such a state; and

(iv) any European Technical Approvals issued in accordance with Directive 89/106/EEC, which give an equivalent standard of protection and performance to the relevant British Standard or British Standard Code of Practice will also be deemed to satisfy the relevant requirements of these Regulations.

These provisions do not preclude use of other methods or materials which will satisfy the functional requirements (A3).

The Regulations provide for the giving of notices to and the deposit of plans and particulars with the appropriate district council. They also make provision (regulation A15) about the exercise of powers of dispensation or relaxation. The functions of a district council with respect to the passing or rejection of plans, and their powers in relation to work which does not conform with building regulations, are set out in the Building Regulations (Northern Ireland) Order 1979 ("the Order").

Two parts (E and H) differ in form from the 1990 Regulations by being more generalised statements of requirements supported by Technical Booklets prepared by the Department of the Environment for Northern Ireland ("DOE (NI) Technical Booklets"). These Booklets contain tables formerly contained in the 1990 Regulations and provide for certain methods and standards of building which, if followed, will be deemed to satisfy the requirements of these Regulations. A further Part (K) also contains a more generalised statement of requirements supplemented by deemed to satisfy provisions set out in that Part itself.

Part EE (Means of Escape in Case of Fire) of the 1990 Regulations has been omitted and its requirements transferred to Part E. Part V (Glazing) has been introduced for the first time.

Apart from the changes referred to above, the principal changes from the 1990 Regulations are–

1. In Part A (Interpretation and general)–

    (a) building work in connection with a wholly or partially exempted building is required to be carried out so as not to create a new or greater contravention of these regulations in any existing building (A5(3));

    (b) certain requirements of Part E and Part K are applied to the provision of a service or fitting (A8);

    (c) revised material change of use cases have been introduced and the relevant requirements are set out in tabular form (A9);

    (d) the Regulations provide for the issue by district councils of a completion certificate specifying where building work carried out on a building or part of a building complies with the requirements of these Regulations (A12); and

    (e) the power of district councils to relax or dispense with these Regulations is extended to include all applications in respect of work to which Part E relates (A15).

2. In Part B (Materials and workmanship) the prohibition of gas supported structures is omitted.

3. In Part C (Preparation of site and resistance to moisture) a new regulation (C2(2)) requires measures to be taken to prevent the ingress of radon from the ground into dwellings that are situated in specified areas (shown on the map in Schedule 4).

4. In Part D (Structure) certain 5-storey buildings are exempt from the requirement relating to disproportionate collapse (D4).

5. In Part E (retitled Fire safety)–

    (a) the requirements for means of escape in case of fire apply to all buildings (E2); and

    (b) access and facilities for the fire brigade are required (E10).

6. In Part G (Sound insulation of dwellings) requirements for walls and floors that become separating walls and separating floors when a new dwelling is created in an existing building are included (G4).

7. In Part H (retitled Stairs, ramps and guarding)–

    (a) there are new requirements controlling stairs, ramps and landings between the entrance or exit of a building and the adjacent ground level (H3); and

    (b) guarding is required to a sunken area next to a building (H5).

8. In Part K (Ventilation) the use of extract ventilation in a kitchen which contains a heat-producing appliance that is not room-sealed is excluded as a deemed-to-satisfy provision in certain circumstances (K3).

9. In Part R (retitled Access and facilities for disabled people)–

    (a) access requirements for disabled people are extended to more building uses (R1); and

    (b) subject to certain exemptions, sanitary accommodation for disabled people is required where any sanitary accommodation is provided (R4).

10. In Part V (Glazing) requirements are introduced to control glazing with which people are likely to come into contact or collide (V1 and V3).

11. In Schedule 1 Part A (Partially exempted buildings) partially exempt status is limited to certain conservatories, greenhouses and porches that are attached to other buildings.

12. In Schedule 1 Part B (Classes of wholly exempted buildings) wholly exempt status is extended to certain covered areas and to many small detached buildings that were partially exempted in the 1990 Regulations.

Explanatory Note

13. In Schedule 2 (Giving of notices and deposit of plans) Rule A requires additional documents to be submitted in respect of buildings or parts of buildings that are put to a designated use for the purposes of the Fire Services (Northern Ireland) Order 1984.

Other minor and consequential amendments have been made including the necessary changes to take account of revised editions of and amendments to DOE (NI) Technical Booklets, British Standards, British Standard Codes of Practice and other publications.

The publications referred to in these Regulations may be purchased from the following source–

British Standards and British Standard Codes of Practice from the Sales Department, British Standards Institution, Linford Wood, Milton Keynes MK14 6LE; and all other publications from branches of Her Majesty's Stationery Office.

If any works to which these Regulations apply contravene these Regulations, the district council in whose area those works are being or have been done may by notice served on the owner under Article 18(1) of the Order require him to pull down or remove those works, or, if he so elects and the council so agrees, to effect such alterations or additions therein as are necessary to make the works comply with the requirements of these Regulations.

Any person who contravenes any provisions contained in these Regulations or a notice under Article 18(1) of the Order is guilty of an offence under the Order and is liable on summary conviction to a fine not exceeding level 5 on the standard scale of fines and penalties (presently £2,000) and to a further fine not exceeding £50 for each day during which the offence continues after conviction therefor.

INDEX OF SUBJECTS

(This index is not part of the Regulations)

Index

Index

Printed in the United Kingdom for the
Controller and Chief Executive of Her Majesty's Stationery Office
being the Officer appointed to print the
Measures of the Northern Ireland Assembly and
published by Her Majesty's Stationery Office

Dd. 8713948. C16. 6/94. Gp. 130. 14567.

£9.50 net